THE SYSTEMS LEADER

"In this dynamic era of reinvention, the AI revolution, and nonstop change, every business leader can benefit from the experience and insights of a trusted advisor. *The Systems Leader* is Robert Siegel at his best—a wise, perceptive, and always practical guide to increasing resilience and agility, driving innovation and creating value."

—Julie Sweet, chair and CEO, Accenture

"Robert Siegel, with his unique blend of practical experience and academic insight, offers a compelling exploration of the challenges facing today's business leaders. Debunking the myth of the infallible leader, he presents a profile of a leader capable of navigating uncertainty and overcoming obstacles with humility and ambition."

—François-Henri Pinault, chairman and CEO, Kering

"In times where the only constant is change, Robert Siegel's new book, *The Systems Leader,* is a brilliant blueprint for navigating the turbulence. Siegel carefully dissects the unprecedented challenges CEOs face, making a compelling case that change is accelerating more rapidly than ever. He proposes a systematic leadership approach to these challenges organized around five major cross-pressures. His observations are based on his own extensive business and academic experience and interviews with dozens of successful business leaders. Although he proposes a systematic way to address challenges, it is refreshing that his approach leaves room for nuance and advocates balance in responding to challenges. This new book is a must-read for leaders in search of practical help to address a myriad of challenges."

—The Honorable Rob Portman, former United States senator (OH)

"Robert Siegel is a dedicated lecturer, operator, and lifelong chronicler of innovation. In *The Systems Leader*, Siegel outlines profound technological and cultural change all leaders must now contend with, and how to preempt and respond to dramatic shifts that affect their daily actions. Siegel knows better than anyone that leadership is not just management; leaders of all kinds can benefit from his wisdom and stories of how to thrive in times of immense uncertainty."

—Katherine Boyle, general partner, Andreessen Horowitz

"Navigating the many complex pressures of modern leadership, Systems Leadership is Robert Siegel's new framework to equip leaders on how to harmonize execution with innovation, balancing stakeholder needs and cultivating a culture of accountability and understanding. This book is essential reading for anyone striving to thrive in today's dynamic business landscape."

—Jochen Zeitz, president, CEO, and chairman, Harley-Davidson

"Robert Siegel has an ability to break through the corporate facades we all present and deliver real insights into the challenges and learnings of a range of leaders. I learn about my own business when speaking with Robert and am delighted to see that I learn from others as well. If we avoid only one mistake or deliver one great insight as a result of reading this book, it's a huge win—and I think there is a lot more than one apiece in this gem."

—Bill Winters, group chief executive, Standard Chartered

"Systems Leadership is a powerful approach that helps leaders integrate challenges that seem like polar opposites (cross-pressures), allowing managers to drive great outcomes rather than make bad trade-offs. Having worked for a Systems Leader at Roblox, I can vouch for the power of the approach as companies navigate short- and long-term challenges in a highly competitive global economy. Robert's writing is infused with great examples and all of the enthusiasm that he brings to the classroom."

—Michael Guthrie, CFO, Roblox

"Leadership today isn't just about hitting targets; it's about thriving amid complexity and driving meaningful change. *The Systems Leader* is a master class in balancing bold innovation with execution. Robert Siegel captures the essence of what it takes to lead in a world where disruption is constant. This is the playbook for leaders who aren't just adapting to change—they're shaping it."

—Dara Treseder, chief marketing officer, Autodesk

"Robert Siegel's new book, *The System Leader,* opens up the dimensions of our complex world with the infinite possibilities and networks of dynamic impact. Robert has beautifully masterminded the framing and reframing of the critical changes of our time with practical approaches for leaders to face these questions. This book provides inspiring insights for anyone interested in the future of leadership."

—Pekka Ala-Pietilä, chairperson of the supervisory board, SAP; former president, Nokia Group

"In this book, Robert Siegel articulately and empathetically summarizes the challenges facing the leaders I work with every day—pressures from rapidly evolving technology, chaotic geopolitics, and changing preferences among employees. But *The Systems Leader* also provides inspiration in the form of a framework for young and old leaders to thrive in this environment, drawing lessons from real-life examples observed throughout the many hats Robert has worn in his career. It's a must-read for anyone aspiring to lead their organizations into the future."

—Sagar Sanghvi, CFO, Abridge; former partner, Accel; and CFO, Instacart

"In this era of constant and unprecedented changes, leaders are tasked not only to manage both the short-term business and long-term strategic goals but also to align the interests of diverse stakeholders both within and outside the organization. Robert Siegel tackles this seemingly impossible task through his latest book, delving into real-life success stories of leading executives, offering insights and thought-provoking perspectives on how leaders can effectively create a harmonious yet accountable workforce and environment. *The Systems Leader* is an essential read for leaders seeking to thoughtfully explore and address the multifaceted demands of leadership today."

—Shigeki Yamaguchi, CEO, NTT DATA Institute of
Management Consulting and QUNIE

THE SYSTEMS LEADER

THE
SYSTEMS
LEADER

Mastering the Cross-Pressures That
Make or Break Today's Companies

ROBERT E. SIEGEL

CROWN
CURRENCY
NEW YORK

CROWN CURRENCY
An imprint of the Crown Publishing Group
A division of Penguin Random House LLC
1745 Broadway
New York, NY 10019
crownpublishing.com
penguinrandomhouse.com

All photographs by the author.

Library of Congress Cataloging-in-Publication Data
Names: Siegel, Robert E., author. Title: The systems leader: mastering the
cross-pressures that make or break today's companies / Robert Siegel. Description:
New York: Crown Currency, [2025] | Includes bibliographical references and index. |
Identifiers: LCCN 2024047918 (print) | LCCN 2024047919 (ebook) |
ISBN 9780593800041 (hardcover) | ISBN 9780593800058 (ebook)
Subjects: LCSH: Leadership. | System analysis. Classification: LCC HD57.7
.S4984 2025 (print) | LCC HD57.7 (ebook) | DDC 658.4/092—dc23/eng/20241011
LC record available at https://lccn.loc.gov/2024047918
LC ebook record available at https://lccn.loc.gov/2024047919

Hardcover ISBN 978-0-593-80004-1
International edition ISBN 979-8-217-08708-2
Ebook ISBN 978-0-593-80005-8

Editor: Paul Whitlatch
Editorial assistant: Katie Berry
Production editor: Patricia Shaw
Text designer: Amani Shakrah
Production: Phil Leung
Copy editor: Anne Cherry
Proofreaders: Lawrence Krauser, Katie McGuire, and Andrea Peabbles
Indexer: Cathy Dorsey
Publicist: Penny Simon
Marketer: Chantelle Walker

Manufactured in the United States of America

1 3 5 7 9 8 6 4 2

First Edition

To my teachers and mentors across the years—
those who paved the way, those who walk beside me,
and those who come after. Your wisdom has been a blessing.

If [we] have seen further, it is by standing on
the shoulders of Giants.

—Sir Isaac Newton, 1675

CONTENTS

The Tide Is Staying Out

The Problem: Even Great Companies Face Cross-Pressures

It's 2:00 PM on a Tuesday in a classroom at Stanford, and I'm standing in front of seventy-five executives who work at companies from all over the world. For the past day and a half, these men and women have been listening to my colleagues speak on aspects of innovation and managing change in their organizations. I suspect that many are wondering what the title of my session, "Systems Leadership," actually means.

My first slide is just a brief quote: "Oh Lord, won't you buy me a Mercedes-Benz?" I ask who recognizes it; about half of the audience raise their hands. The rest learn that it's the first line of Janis Joplin's classic 1971 song, "Mercedes-Benz." Then I show these pictures I took in Stuttgart, Germany:

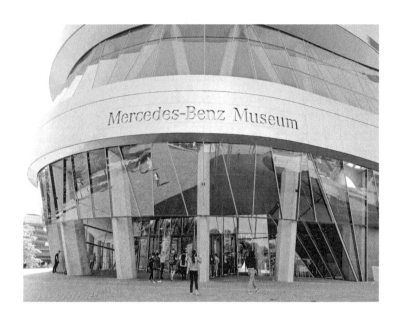

I tell them that 800,000 people a year visit the Mercedes-Benz Museum to admire hundreds of beautiful, historic cars, some of which go back to the company's origins in the 1890s. I ask the room: "How many of you wish your company was so universally known and widely loved that rock stars would write songs about you and tourists would go out of their way to see your corporate museum?" Every hand flies up.

"Mercedes-Benz* has all the advantages any company could dream of. It has one of the world's most prestigious global brands. It has premium pricing power. It employs many of the industry's most talented engineers and designers. It has superfans who won't even consider driving other kinds of cars."

Then I throw a curveball: "But despite all of those advantages, this iconic company is facing serious challenges."

I go through some details from a Stanford University case study about the transition from gasoline-powered to electric vehicles, the rise of autonomous driving, the connectivity and digitization of the automobile, and the global boom in ride-sharing—all of which might pose existential threats to Mercedes-Benz. Of course the company's leaders are investing in EV models; every automaker on Earth is doing that. They are also investing in software and autonomous driving. But the big questions are *how much* they should be investing and *how quickly* they should try to nudge their customers toward EVs and other innovations. Every dollar (or in this case, euro) invested in the future equals less profit this year.

I ask the room to predict how long it will take for these trends to

---

* In 2022, the company known as Daimler split in two, spinning off its truck business as Daimler Truck. The car company is now called The Mercedes-Benz Group AG, or simply "Mercedes-Benz" in casual use.

become existential threats to the company. We do a series of raised hands for different time frames; most think it will take ten to fifteen years. Then I point out that the average Fortune Global 250 CEO serves only 4.5 years and is compensated mainly via stock grants and stock options—whose value is largely tied to near-term growth and profits. Suddenly, what seemed like a no-brainer priority to go full speed ahead on innovation is a lot more complicated.

I ask them to imagine being members of the Mercedes-Benz senior executive team. "Would you tell the CEO that these changes to the industry are existential threats, or merely evolutionary steps that can be managed without making radical changes? If they *are* existential, how much annual profit are you willing to sacrifice to catch up with Tesla and BYD? Which aspects of these transformations, such as software or batteries, would you design from scratch and own exclusively, even if that requires building entirely new competencies? Which aspects would you buy from partners, even if that means sacrificing some control and uniqueness? Is it safe to create a supply chain for building EVs in China, or would it be safer to refit some of your factories in Germany, even if that costs more? Would you focus on the large market for $30,000 EVs, like we see coming out of China, or the narrower market for $80,000 EVs?"

These questions epitomize the concept of *cross-pressure*—that is, pressure to achieve seemingly contradictory goals at the same time. In this case, the leaders of Mercedes-Benz feel they must hit their profit targets this year without falling behind competitors in five years. Navigating these kinds of cross-pressures is *hard,* I tell my audience of executives. It's hard if you have one of the world's greatest brands. And it's even harder if you don't.

As the session continues, I see that the room has perked up. People are nodding and engaging attentively. They know they need help because they, too, face cross-pressures in their own companies—more so with each passing year.

The Context: Permanent Low Tide

Warren Buffett famously said, "It's only when the tide goes out that you learn who's been swimming naked." He was referring to economic cycles, which inevitably (if unpredictably) move through booms and busts. In some years, it seems like any businessperson can find success due to a healthy economy; in other years, the naked swimmers are exposed and humiliated. But leadership—actually running companies, departments, business units, or other organizations—is independent of cycles. When times get especially tough, leaders can't count on the tide returning anytime soon. They might be facing powerful, compounding forces that will make it exceptionally difficult to fulfill their missions for years to come.

Since the start of this century, businesses have confronted a host of extreme disruptions and transitions, including technological upheavals, economic instability, geopolitical conflicts and wars, a worldwide pandemic, a global financial crisis, the increasing rise of activist investors, and fundamental changes in the socioeconomic structure of society. While business leaders in every era of modern history have faced disruptions, we've never before seen such a constant, unrelenting, and diverse blend of them.

Today's leaders at all levels, from new startups to global giants, face cross-pressures from their bosses, investors, customers, peers, suppliers, and employees that their predecessors never did. And these stakeholders are sometimes far from aligned. Leaders face pressure to do opposing things at the same time, which can make them feel like no matter what they do or how well they do it, they are getting it all wrong. And these cross-pressures, while acutely felt, are rarely articulated in a way that makes them graspable and actionable.

I've seen the impact of these cross-pressures firsthand—both as a teacher and a business practitioner. As a Lecturer in Management at Stanford's Graduate School of Business, I host global CEOs and prominent executives who provide insights to my students about running real-world organizations. As an investor in startups around the world, I talk to entrepreneurs struggling to find clarity in the chaos of conflicting tensions. And as a consultant and executive education teacher, I see countless teams of managers, at all sorts of companies, struggling for a path forward.

CEOs are far from the only ones feeling such cross-pressures. I've heard similar frustrations from a wide range of middle managers, business unit leaders, and entrepreneurs. The principles and rules of thumb that once guided them now seem less and less useful. These days it often feels like Warren Buffett's tide is staying out, with no hint of when it might return.

I have good news for them.

The Solution: Systems Leadership

I've spent the last eight years developing a new leadership framework in collaboration with Jeff Immelt, former CEO of General Electric. We call it Systems Leadership, and we've shared it not only with the students we coteach at Stanford but also with my consulting and executive education clients, with startup teams, and with leaders of all stripes. As you'll see in chapter 2, it's a "third way" that contrasts with both traditional, command-and-control leadership and disruptive, Silicon Valley–style leadership.

We came up with the name as a play on "systems thinking," a phrase technologists often use. Systems thinking was made popular by Peter Senge in his influential 1990 book, *The Fifth Discipline*. Senge emphasized the interplay of actions and reactions between components of any kind of system, and the importance of studying those relationships holistically, not as isolated parts. Whether one is trying to improve a car engine, heal a sick patient, or predict the weather, there are significant limitations to focusing on a single component rather than on the complex, simultaneous interactions of multiple forces.

Thus, Jeff and I approached leadership not as a collection of discrete skills that one could learn in separate courses (finance, marketing, operations, and so on), but as a holistic, interdisciplinary path to figuring out the right things to do and then consistently accomplishing those goals. Systems Leadership includes strategies to balance short-term execution and long-term innovation, the needs of both internal and external stakeholders, holding employees accountable while treating them with respect and empathy, and much more.

Systems Leadership resonates with virtually everyone I explain it to, because it gives leaders at all levels and in all industries a new language to discuss their biggest pain points and toughest trade-offs. It shows them how to address the cross-pressures they feel, instead of trying to wish away, steamroll, or run from them. It empowers them to be proactive instead of reactive, which helps them feel more in control of their own fate. It offers them a playbook for riding turbulent waves without drowning. In short, it takes them from chaos to clarity.

We'll get into the details soon, but the gist of Systems Leadership is reframing and learning how to master five key dimensions of cross-pressures that I've gleaned from years of studying and interviewing leaders. These dimensions are:

- *Priorities:* The need to succeed at both execution *and* innovation

- *People:* The need to project both strength *and* empathy

- *Sphere of influence:* The need to focus both internally *and* externally

- *Geography:* The need to think both locally *and* globally

- *Purpose:* The need to pursue both ambition *and* statesmanship

These pressures, of course, don't exist in silos. I believe the interdependence of these cross-pressures is a major reason why they feel so frustrating and complex. For instance, how you balance execution today and innovation for tomorrow affects how you manage your people, and vice versa. How you deal with both internal and external stakeholders is shaped by your company's purpose, and the reverse is also true.

Fair warning: Systems Leadership is not a magic bullet. I understand the appeal of books that claim to offer simple answers to complex challenges. But in my decades in business and academia, I have never seen any specific strategies or tactics that are *guaranteed* to elevate a company or career. Systems Leadership begins with embracing how much you *don't* know at any given moment, and gives you a way to move forward with reasonable confidence but not delusional overconfidence. It's only human to crave certainty, but true leaders accept that much of business (and life) depends on both contingencies and luck. You can make great decisions that factor in all the relevant probabilities but still get terrible results. Even clueless leaders can look like geniuses when times are good.

This need for humility is especially true with respect to the five primary cross-pressures. For instance, it's easy for me to say that you need to focus on both executing your current business plan *and* innovating for the future, but what does that mean in practice? Your time and energy are extremely limited, so how much of them should you devote to product development or other forms of innovation? I wouldn't presume to tell you whether it's 20 percent or 80 percent or anywhere in between. Nor will I make up some formula to decide for you. Instead, I offer a framework for you to do some well-informed wrestling with such trade-offs yourself, along with stories of how some of the best leaders I know have wrestled with them.

The Interviewees

In this book I will introduce you to a wide range of impressive leaders who have found themselves facing these turbulent cross-pressures in their roles. No one gets it right all the time, and it's overly simplistic to divide leaders into sharp categories of winners and losers. For instance, Jeff Immelt worked at GE for thirty-five years, including sixteen as CEO. During most of that time he was hailed as one of the best corporate executives in the world—until he was widely blamed for all of his company's problems. The truth is that he was neither perfect nor terrible; he was a talented CEO who did his best to confront extreme cross-pressures, many of them created by forces beyond his control, and others through his own choices.

The Systems Leaders I've interviewed have climbed to the top echelons of their fields. They generally opened up to me with great candor, in conversations that went far beyond typical CEO interviews about new products and projected growth. Among those you'll get to know:

- Revathi Advaithi at Flex

- Naomi Allen at Brightline Heath

- Michael Dowling at Northwell Health

- Jim Fish at Waste Management

- Aaron Levie at Box

- Kathy Mazzarella at Graybar

- Khaldoon Al Mubarak at Mubadala

- François-Henri Pinault at Kering

- Charlie Scharf at Wells Fargo

- Julie Sweet at Accenture

- Bill Winters at Standard Chartered

- Anne Wojcicki at 23andMe

- Jochen Zeitz at Harley-Davidson

What unites these and other diverse Systems Leaders is that none claim to be heroic role models whom the rest of us should emulate. They all face nonstop ambiguities, uncertainties, and problems that have no clear solution. They all recognize and admit that they don't get every decision right. Yet they all have a lot to teach us—not *what* to think, but *how* to think about our own unique situations.

Where I'm Coming From

Since we all have biases shaped by our experiences, I should tell you a bit more about myself before we continue.

One of my first jobs after college and graduate school was at Intel during its glory days as a foundational player in the personal computer revolution of the 1990s. I was fortunate to serve as a manager in the company's Corporate Business Development group, and then as a product manager in a business unit. I also had the good luck to work closely with our legendary CEO, Andy Grove, who in retrospect was a Systems Leader decades before we envisioned that concept. Andy was one of the most driven and brilliant leaders I've ever met, a master of everything from running a high-tech factory efficiently to understanding global interdependencies. (I remember him saying in 1993, in regard to the United States and China, that no country will ever go to war with another if that's where they place their factories. His insights have held up for more than three decades, even through increasing geopolitical tensions.)

After leaving Intel in 1998, I founded one startup and was an executive in another; I would later return to the tech startup world as an early-stage venture capital investor and an adviser to founders. Those roles gave me new perspectives on the ways that startup leadership is both similar to and extremely different from corporate leadership. It was exciting to work with visionaries who embraced cutting-edge technologies and wanted to change the world. But just like big companies, startups could only survive if they got good at the practical details of delivering goods and services, on time and on budget.

Along the way, I did a stint at another famous global corporation, General Electric. GE taught me the importance of people development and how an exceptional investment in talent can be a huge competitive advantage, increasing loyalty while building a deep bench of new leaders. GE also trained me to appreciate the executional rigor required to manufacture high-quality goods in high volumes around the globe. A commitment to both excellence and scale ran throughout the organization.

Meanwhile, in 2003, I started teaching and researching at the Stanford Graduate School of Business, which gave me yet another way of seeing the world. My experiences as an operating executive, investor, consultant, and board member helped me be a better teacher, while the insights I gained from studying and writing about companies with academic detachment helped in my other roles. As I have increased my activities and taught nine different courses at Stanford over the years, I've gotten to know companies across different geographies, industries, and stages, and I've observed the best (and worst) practices of many organizations.

After wearing all these hats, I like to think I can offer a perspective on highly effective leadership. And I'm passionate about sharing what I have learned.

What's Ahead

Here's what you can expect in the pages ahead.

Part 1 will give you deeper understanding of the perfect storm of unprecedented forces now causing chaos at many organizations. It shows the grim consequences faced by leaders who failed to respond to those challenges with appropriate thoughtfulness and gravitas. Then the book turns to introducing the concept of Systems Leadership and some of the amazing men and women who already apply it, even if they don't use that terminology.

Part 2 digs more deeply into the five major cross-pressures that tend to recur—priorities, people, sphere of influence, geography, and purpose—and strategies for navigating them. It also highlights the fascinating, candid, sometimes deeply personal stories of my interviewees, many of which have never been shared publicly until now.

By the time you finish the book, I hope you'll agree that even though running any kind of business is harder than ever in many ways, great leadership is still both possible and worth the effort. If you want to improve your corner of the world while also reaching your personal and professional goals, I can't think of a better strategy than studying and practicing Systems Leadership.

PART 1

Why Is Leadership So Hard These Days?

CHAPTER 1

The Perfect Storm of Chaotic Forces

Pulled in Opposite Directions

In the mid-2000s I ran the video surveillance division of GE Security—one of the most rewarding leadership roles I've ever held. We made high-quality cameras and video recording equipment for companies that needed to protect their operations. It was a strong B2B model, with great people, steady growth, and reliable profitability. There was just one problem: our industry was about to transform from analog to digital video. You didn't need to be a futurist to see that digital was on the path to becoming both cheaper and more convenient. If my unit didn't get a jump on that transition, it wouldn't matter how much our customers liked us or how much they trusted the GE brand. They'd switch to another vendor for video surveillance.

We needed to offer a high-end digital video management system, which is basically a complex software overlay that controls networked cameras, the recording process, and the storage of digital video. We could either build our own proprietary system or acquire one from an independent company. This was a classic "make or buy" problem that almost every company confronts at some point and learns to evaluate. By my math, it would take six quarters to build and launch a digital offering (perhaps twice as long as it would take to buy one), and we'd have to invest roughly $2.5 million of our $19 million quarterly profit for each of the six quarters. But that would still be cheaper than buying someone else's system, and it would give us the freedom to control quality and features. The investment seemed like a no-brainer to maintain our lead in the market.

When I explained the situation to my boss, however, I learned that it wasn't so simple. He said that if I wanted to spend an additional $2.5 million per quarter on R&D, I'd need to come up with an extra $5 million in revenue to make up for it, so our profit wouldn't take a hit. I replied that if I had an easy way to sell another $5 million of product per quarter, wouldn't we already be doing it? I stressed that if we stuck with our status quo offerings, this year's numbers would still be strong, but we'd start bleeding customers within eighteen to twenty-four months.

We danced around this topic for more than an hour, as I tried to convince my boss that this was a necessary—even existential—step for our business. He kept challenging me to find some other way to pay for it. If the world was changing, it was my responsibility to sustain our current profits while also finding more money to pay for the investment.

Finally, my boss shook his head and firmly said, "Rob, you're missing the point. In eighteen months, you and I will both be in different jobs. And the way for you to get a *better* new job is to hit your targets this year. The CFO is counting on your profits to subsidize other divisions that underperform. If you spend all that money on R&D, you and I will take the pain this year, but we'll get none of the benefit in two years when revenue comes in. By then you and I will be in different roles."

I was simultaneously stunned, perplexed, and angry. How had my boss become so short-sighted? Weren't leaders like us expected to pursue long-term domination of our markets? Why were my personal incentives misaligned with GE's best interests? Why couldn't we find a way to execute now while still innovating for the future?

Long story short, my unit didn't invest in the digital transition, and I left GE a few months later. One reason I departed was my frustration that the balance between short-term and long-term priorities in my division had gotten out of whack. I hated feeling pulled in opposite directions.

About eighteen months after I resigned, I got a surprise call from the senior executive at GE who had replaced my former boss shortly before my departure. We hadn't worked together long and weren't close, but Jerry was a thoughtful and considerate leader. He told me that the scenario I'd predicted was coming true; the video surveillance unit had already lost half its revenue to competitors with digital offerings. "We should have listened to what you said before you left."

I replied, "Jerry, I really appreciate the update. But I didn't want to be right—I wanted us to win. I wanted us to do the right thing. It still breaks my heart that the company couldn't get it done, and I feel like I failed because I couldn't convince people to go with the plan."

I didn't have a name for my experience at the time, but the dynamic I encountered at GE was a classic cross-pressure. The top leaders talked about investing for the future, but other parts of the company signaled that short-term financial targets were the true priority. The unspoken culture was that leaders who missed their numbers lost their jobs, but if you found a way to ignore the problem, you could pass the buck to someone else.

Another thing I didn't realize at the time was that such cross-pressures were becoming both more common and more intense, for all sorts of leaders around the world.

Future Shock on Steroids

A book that has stuck in my head for many years is Alvin Toffler's *Future Shock*, the 1970 bestseller about the forces transforming the world. He argued that the rate of change of different aspects of modern life—technological, economic, and social—had accelerated beyond the human capacity to adapt to those changes. As a result, Toffler predicted drastic upheavals in how we all lived and worked. He was decades ahead of his time in foreseeing the boom in personal computers, migration into cities, and fast fashion. He even popularized the phrase *information overload* to stress that humans weren't built to handle the modern flood of continuous inputs.

It's ironic that from the perspective of the 2020s, Toffler's era looks calm and peaceful, a paradise of easily manageable information flows. Those of us who began our careers before ubiquitous cell phones, email, and texting can get nostalgic for leaving work fully behind at the end of each day. The limits of technology enforced a de facto work-life boundary; almost no boss would call us at home except in a true emergency. So I wasn't surprised when a 2023 poll found that "most Americans would prefer to live in a simpler era before everyone was obsessed with screens and social media, and this sentiment is especially strong among older Millennials and Gen Xers. Asked whether they would like to return to a time before . . . people had wide access to the internet and smartphones, 77% of Americans aged 35–54 said they would."[1]

Despite his foresight, even Toffler couldn't have predicted the stunning acceleration of technological change since roughly the year 2000. Every piece of data that *could be* digitized *has been* digitized. Every product that *could be* upgraded by adding microchips, Radio Frequency Identification (RFID), and/or GPS *has been* upgraded. Robotics and artificial intelligence are improving every month. Cybersecurity is becoming a bigger and more complex challenge. Even accidental glitches, like the global computer outage caused by a faulty CrowdStrike software update in July 2024, now have bigger consequences than ever before. Staying on top of these and other technological changes, as well as knowing how to deploy resources to address them, can be overwhelming for most businesspeople.

You've probably seen a graph similar to the one on the next page, showing the steadily increasing pace of mass adoption of transformative technologies.[2] Whereas it took almost fifty years for a quarter of Americans to have used electricity, more than thirty-five years for the telephone, and twenty-five years for television, it took less than three years for more than 25 percent of the U.S. population to use Generative AI. How much shorter will future lines be for other innovations that are still ramping up? We're living through *Future Shock* on steroids.

Moreover, tech innovation is only one of multiple forces that can contribute to a widespread sense of dislocation and unease. And those other forces have also accelerated in this century—arguably just as rapidly and distressingly as technology has accelerated. A piece in *The Guardian* in December 2019 offered a pithy and dismal summary of the 2010s: "There have been crises of democracy and the economy; of the climate and poverty; of international relations and national identity; of privacy and technology. There were crises at the start of the decade, and there are crises now. Some of them are the same crises, unsolved. Others are like nothing we have experienced before. . . . It has often felt as if everything is up for

Generative AI Has a Steeper Initial Adoption Curve Than Other Recent Technologies

millions U.S. users

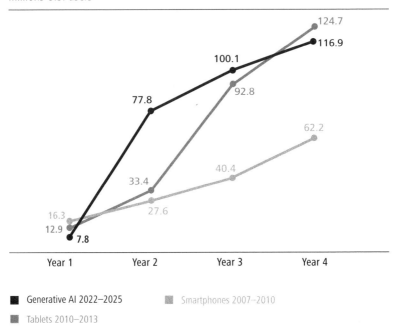

Legend:
- ■ Generative AI 2022–2025
- ■ Smartphones 2007–2010
- ■ Tablets 2010–2013

Note: Individuals of any age who use each technology at least once per month; Year 1 for smartphones corresponds with the June 2007 release of the iPhone; Year 1 for tablets corresponds with the April 2010 release of the iPad; Year 1 of generative AI corresponds with the November 2022 release of ChatGPT

Source: Insider Intelligence, June 2023

grabs—from the future of capitalism to the future of the planet—and yet nothing has been decided."[3]

We can sort these *nontechnological* upheavals into several distinct buckets:

- *Economic dislocation.* We've experienced a nearly nonstop economic roller coaster—from the dotcom crash to the bubble of the mid-2000s; to the global financial crisis and

the worst recession since the Great Depression; to the
uneven economic growth of the 2010s, with prosperity
seemingly concentrated in only a few industries and areas;
to the COVID supply shocks and layoffs; to the return of
significant inflation.

- *Ubiquitous globalization.* Not so long ago, it was almost
  exclusively giant corporations that had to figure out how to
  do business internationally. But today even small startups
  feel pressure to seek supply chains and customer bases
  across borders and oceans, which exposes them to complex
  international issues and unanticipated risks. With the
  growth of communication and collaboration tools, even
  small companies can sell internationally in ways previously
  not possible.

- *Political instability.* For all the downsides of the Cold War
  era, at least it offered a degree of predictability in
  international and domestic politics. But our century has
  seen greater political instability worldwide, including the
  rise of various extreme movements and even small
  countries willing to curtail democratic processes to
  achieve their goals and upend the international order.
  Such instability makes everything harder for business
  leaders.

- *Changing labor force dynamics.* Generational attitudes
  toward work are substantively different from the past.
  Newcomers to the working world generally used to accept
  the norms of their elders, even if they quietly disagreed
  with those norms. But Millennials and especially Gen Z
  have been far more outspoken about what they expect from
  employers and how they expect to be treated.

- *Changing expectations on social issues.* Workers have pushed companies to take public positions on societal challenges, reversing the traditional norm that most companies would avoid politics and controversial debates (such as abortion rights) to focus on their own business imperatives. Even if there has been some rebalancing of expectations on companies speaking up on social issues over the last couple of years, the business environment is very different today than ten or twenty years ago.

- *Changing expectations for personal development.* Another norm that has seemingly changed forever is that employees used to be responsible for their own work-life balance, career development, and personal needs. Now managers are increasingly expected to pay close attention to such matters for their teams, or face significant disapproval.

- *"Black swan" shocks.* One major lesson of the pandemic was that virtually all leaders, in both the public and private sectors, were unprepared for a prolonged, unexpected disruption to the status quo. In general, we've gotten much better in recent decades at modeling predictable trends, but not at anticipating extremely rare "black swan" events, to use the term popularized by Nassim Nicholas Taleb.[4] We also learned that such shocks are especially vexing if they require collective action across many public and private organizations, on a global scale.

- *Conflicts over climate change.* Science shows that the climate is always changing, with acceleration in the last few decades. We're still not sure just how bad climate change will get, or how quickly, or how public and private institutions will respond to its global impacts. For instance, what will happen to international refugee processes if some coastal countries are underwater in thirty years? What if half of Florida is submerged in fifty years? It's only human to want to avoid thinking about such scenarios, let alone planning for them. Yet, while many now feel passionate about doing whatever it takes to slow climate change, many in the developing world feel equally passionate about not sacrificing recent gains in their standard of living by giving up fossil fuels. That's a recipe for inevitable tensions and conflicts.

▪ *Changing financial markets.* For companies with publicly traded stock, pressures from activist investors and pundits to justify corporate activities on issues such as ESG and DEI are very different from the past. And the speed with which attitudes toward these topics can change is a real challenge for company leaders. Nowadays influential investors can take to social media seeking to shift public opinion on companies they target. There's also the new risk of suddenly becoming a meme stock, a position that companies like AMC and Hertz found themselves in during the COVID pandemic. For privately held companies, the pressure to become a "unicorn" (valued at over $1 billion) in a quick time horizon has driven leaders to take on vast amounts of venture capital to grow at extremely accelerated, sometimes irresponsible rates.

When you stop to consider all of these potential disruptions, the notion of leading a company seems like a minefield. I don't mean to imply that it used to be *easy* to lead a business during

Toffler's era, or any prior era. Each generation faces its own disruptions, some of them massively challenging. It's not helpful to look backward with too much rose-colored nostalgia. Nevertheless, what's truly different now is that we've never before seen such a sustained and unrelenting combination of disruptive forces. Most of today's leaders have not been trained in, nor had time to think deeply about, such an array of complex challenges, which go far beyond the scope of traditional business education.

How This Perfect Storm Drives Cross-Pressures on Leaders

As diverse as all these forces are, one thing they have in common is that they render traditional rules obsolete. Whether the question is how to raise capital, innovate, launch products, attract and retain talent, market to new users, provide customer service, or interact with suppliers and competitors, practices that worked five or ten years ago may now be inoperative. Whatever "new normal" follows a disruption is never the same as what you knew before. That's easy enough to grasp intellectually; the hard part is truly accepting that some old rules need to be permanently retired—and then figuring out what should replace them.

When you face increasing demands from your bosses, investors, customers, peers, suppliers, and employees, but you no longer know how to satisfy those demands, every day can feel as stressful as running through a maze and never finding an exit. This is especially true when some of those demands seem to require doing opposing things at the same time.

The *Financial Times* recognized this unprecedented situation in a 2023 editorial titled "Who Wants to Be a Modern CEO?" Its observations apply to leaders at all levels: "Consider the plates the modern chief executive must keep spinning. As well as dealing with geopolitical uncertainty, mounting government regulation, high inflation and interest rates, there is rising populism, cyber-attacks and advances in artificial intelligence. Then there is managing reputation risk—including compliance with arduous governance codes—disclosure requirements and pledges on sustainability. Hybrid working brings another set of pressures. And keeping staff motivated and loyal is a full-time job in itself. . . . The pressure is constant to do and say the 'right' thing."[5]

The editorial added that these pressures are exacerbated by much closer scrutiny of executive compensation and conduct, by employees, shareholders, the media, and the public, and "when mistakes are made the reckoning is swift." Such increased scrutiny is a major reason why the median tenure of an S&P 500 CEO fell by 20 percent between 2013 and 2022.[6]

To simplify my analysis of how Systems Leaders keep all these plates spinning successfully, I've focused on five major categories of cross-pressures. Someone else might divide them into more categories, but I find these to be most useful in looking at the challenges that now confront leaders at any level, in any sector:

- *Priorities:* Pressure to succeed at both execution *and* innovation

- *People:* Pressure to project both strength *and* empathy

- *Sphere of influence:* Pressure to focus both internally *and* externally

- *Geography:* Pressure to think both locally *and* globally

- *Purpose:* Pressure to pursue both ambition *and* statesmanship

Let's look more closely at how these cross-pressures can develop and some examples of what they do to leaders in the hot seat.

Priorities: "It's a Lot Harder Now"

The cross-pressure I faced at GE's video surveillance unit in the story at the start of this chapter is extremely widespread, affecting every organization that needs to make hard choices today to preserve viability for tomorrow. While the topic of corporate innovation and reinvention is not new, the pressures, speed, and manners of innovation have changed in our increasingly connected world.

My former Intel boss Andy Grove wrote a bestselling book whose title became an aphorism: *Only the Paranoid Survive.* His main point was that sooner or later, most companies face a "strategic inflection point" when they can either adapt and potentially grow tenfold or fail to adapt and face decline or doom. Recognizing those critical moments is a valuable skill; having the courage to act on them is even more rare and even more valuable. They were relatively infrequent in Grove's era but are now more commonplace.

Anne Wojcicki, cofounder and CEO of 23andMe since 2006, talked to me about the two sides of her company and the cross-pressures between them. 23andMe is best known for the DNA home-testing kits that it produces and processes for millions of individuals—a steady but slow-growth consumer business. But it also uses its unmatched archive of genomic data to perform advanced biotechnology research, a far riskier but potentially much more rewarding endeavor. Wojcicki spearheaded an ambitious partnership in 2018 with pharmaceutical giant GSK, which has made it possible to study the genetic health markers of millions of users to develop cutting-edge treatments for serious diseases.

Commercializing such innovations can take many years to pay off, and many will never succeed at all.

Wojcicki took the company public in 2021, and she explained that because institutional investors evaluate risk in buckets, the company has attracted two distinct categories of risk takers as investors. "People who like our consumer business tend not to like our speculative therapeutics business, while those who like the growth potential of our therapeutics business have no interest in steady cash flow from a consumer business."[7] The two sides of the company combine to deliver strategic and operational synergies, but the cross-pressures make investor relations complicated. Wojcicki faced constant pressure to favor one side over the other, or to split them into separate companies, even though that would hurt their aggregate results.

Those pressures increased significantly after 23andMe went public, making its stock price a daily scorecard. In chapter 4 we'll explore the existential challenges that created for her and the company, and what Wojcicki attempted to do about those challenges.

People: "We Can't Have Blinders On"

In today's increasingly complex environment, leaders often hear two contradictory views on managing talent. One generally argues that tough times call for tough choices, so you should set high standards and clear rules for your people and enforce them rigorously and consistently. Insist on hard work and dedication to excel in your market. Push the team to give 100 percent and "coach out" anyone who is unwilling to comply with these norms.

The other strain of advice stresses that modern employees, especially Millennials and Gen Z, expect their leaders to show empathy and compassion, and even display vulnerability about their own struggles and shortcomings. Furthermore, good leaders and companies should offer generous benefits, lots of remote work, industry-leading salaries, and generous PTO for mental health days—while enforcing as few rules as possible. The cofounders of Basecamp wrote in their 2010 bestseller, *Rework,* that "Policies are organizational scar tissue. They are codified overreactions to situations that are unlikely to happen again. . . . Don't create a policy because one person did something wrong once."[8]

If the goal is leading people effectively, neither extreme works. Tough bosses get scorched on social media, especially on platforms like Blind or Fishbowl that allow employees to complain anonymously about bad treatment (real, exaggerated, or imagined). For instance, when Wayfair CEO Niraj Shah sent out an all-hands email at the end of 2023, praising the furniture retailer's progress but warning that employees should expect to work long hours and "think of any company money you spend as your own," the response was overwhelmingly negative. After several rounds of layoffs that year, surviving Wayfair employees didn't appreciate Shah's tough-love advice. They mocked statements such as "Working long hours, being responsive, blending work and life, is not anything to shy away from. There is not a lot of history of laziness being rewarded with success."[9]

On the other hand, leaders who see themselves as empathetic and benevolent can be in for a rude awakening when employees fail to share the same perception. Consider longtime Starbucks CEO Howard Schultz, who became a target of accusations by union organizers that he unfairly suppressed attempts at collective bargaining. As *The New York Times* reported, "Mr. Schultz's resistance to a union appears to be a matter of self-image, according to those who know him: He prefers to see himself as a generous boss, not a boss who is forced to treat employees generously."[10] Schultz himself wrote in his first memoir, "If they had faith in me and my motives, they wouldn't need a union."[11]

Revathi Advaithi wrestles with this cross-pressure as CEO of Flex, the global technology, supply chain, and manufacturing solutions company. Any contract manufacturer lives and dies on operational excellence; margins can be so thin that every penny matters. But her need to manage her P&L sometimes collides with Advaithi's desire to protect her global workforce of 140,000-plus. She doesn't want to forget the people on the shop floor who form the backbone of manufacturing while making room for experts in advanced robotics, additive manufacturing, and other advanced manufacturing technologies that improve efficiency and lower costs. In particular, she cares about preserving jobs in the United States, the country that gave her so much opportunity as an immigrant from India, which is why she took a hands-on role with the future of domestic manufacturing, joining President Joe Biden's Advisory Committee on Supply Chain Competitiveness in 2022 and the Advisory Committee for Trade Policy and Negotiations in 2023.

Asked about this tension around adopting new technologies like artificial intelligence, machine learning, and automation, Advaithi replied, "We can't have blinders on and say that this doesn't exist, and this is not coming towards us. If you want manufacturing to survive and do well in countries that don't have the free capital that countries like China provide, you have to build a very efficient, integrated combination of hardware and software that draws on the latest technology."[12] In chapter 5 we'll see how Flex is leveraging such technology in a way that empowers its existing workforce.

Sphere of Influence: "Confidence and Reputation Really Do Matter"

We all have specific competencies that play to our strengths. Some leaders are identified early in their careers as being exceptionally good at external challenges, which include communicating effectively with customers, investors, suppliers, and the media. Others seem to have exceptional skill at focusing internally—making the trains run on time, controlling expenses prudently, or keeping the factories humming. Becoming known for specialized skills, as either an "outside" or "inside" leader, was traditionally a good way to move up to the highest levels of an organization.

But that distinction between internal and external spheres of influence is increasingly breaking down, not just at the C-suite level but throughout every organization. Things that happen inside and outside increasingly influence each other in more subtle and complex ways, creating pressures to try to master both at once. For instance, incentives that a company's sales force gives to customers can radically impact the demands on production. Replacing a component in a product to shave ten cents off the unit cost might create glitches that alienate customers. Designing a successful marketing campaign now requires blending high-quality internal data with an external feel for customer motivations.

Today it's crucial to understand what's going on both inside and outside, because every detail is more interconnected than ever. It's hard for engineers to build great products if they never talk to customers, but it's equally hard for sales and marketing people to make a persuasive case to customers if they've never spoken to product designers.

Charlie Scharf faces a particularly acute sphere-of-influence cross-pressure. He became CEO of Wells Fargo in 2019, when the financial giant was dealing with multiple government investigations and enforcement actions, due to past company practices. He also inherited a culture suffering from multiple issues, including a largely demoralized group of executives and managers. COVID and the turmoil that then began hitting regional banks amplified those problems. Since day one, Scharf has confronted serious external challenges from regulators who keep Wells Fargo on a short leash, while simultaneously trying to reform and inspire his workforce of over 200,000.

"When I got here, it was very important that everyone understood the gravity of the situation. It felt like we were in a war, not business as usual. There's still a lot of pressure every day. It's rare for a week to go by when we don't get some call from a regulator or legislator. On top of that, during COVID we went from earning $20 billion a year to $4 billion a year. And therefore we needed to make serious changes in the organization."[13]

These changes began by thinking beyond the company's internal needs and focusing more on the outside world. "Until 2018 we had great financial performance, but our leaders acted as if they had total disregard for our regulators. We didn't care about things that were important to our communities. But the moment there was a problem inside the company, many outside stakeholders turned against us. I said in my first shareholder letter that we're the perfect example of why it's important to think about stakeholders, not just shareholders. In our industry especially, confidence and reputation really do matter. You can't just run an advertising campaign saying that you're a great company." We'll see how Scharf confronted this cross-pressure in chapter 6.

Geography: "We Need to Be Relevant in Each Country"

I find it helpful to distinguish between the "globalization 1.0" of the eighties and nineties and the "globalization 2.0" of our current century. When long-distance shipping first became more practical and affordable, many American companies saw the offshoring of jobs primarily in terms of labor arbitrage. They could replace high-paying, often unionized jobs in the United States with low-cost manufacturing in Asia, low-cost engineering in Eastern Europe, and low-cost customer service in India. The benefits were fairly straightforward to calculate. In fact, many thought that this interconnected world would lead to rising wages for all and bring increased geopolitical stability and peace.

Globalization 2.0 is far more complex, with more opportunities to find customers as well as workers in distant parts of the world, but also far more challenges. Instead of having a company's top leadership concentrated in a single headquarters, with foreign outposts taking orders via a hub-and-spoke model, we've begun to see more organizations operate with a mesh network model.* Independent centers of excellence and innovation in different countries can act as peers with equal clout, or close to it. And they can adapt to the specific needs of customers and employees in each local market.

This evolution puts increasing pressure on leaders to become masters of both local dynamics in their home markets and the cultures, laws, and social trends that can influence production and consumption in many other markets. This dual requirement can become very tough, especially when doing business in complex environments such as China or the Middle East.

I discussed this duality with François-Henri Pinault, chairman

---

* In a mesh network, nodes or points connect to each other directly, dynamically, and nonhierarchically, rather than through a central hub. The idea is that each node acts as a peer with all the others. In the example above, different locations within a company are of equal stature and influence, in contrast to a traditional "headquarters and remote sites" relationship.

and CEO of the luxury fashion conglomerate Kering, which owns a lineup of elite global brands including Gucci, Balenciaga, Saint Laurent, Alexander McQueen, and Brioni. All are renowned for distinctive styles and exceptional craftsmanship; they enjoy high consumer awareness and premium pricing power. One might assume that leading a portfolio of such beloved brands would be easy. But doing so actually requires a constant balancing act between making centralized decisions from Kering's Paris headquarters and delegating authority to the creatives and business leaders of the individual brands around the world. Kering faces persistent cross-pressure between the benefits and challenges of globalization.

For instance, one of Pinault's biggest challenges (and opportunities) is doing business in China. The good news is that over the past decade many Chinese consumers have been obsessed with Kering's brands, and an increasing number had the resources to afford their products. On the other hand, fake knockoff goods remain a big problem.

In chapter 7 we'll see how Kering approaches this balancing act in more than thirty-five countries. As Pinault observed, "It can be very difficult to understand how to reposition a brand to make it relevant in the United States, South America, China, Korea, and Japan, without losing its consistency. We don't want to be different from one country to another, but we need to be relevant in each country."[14]

Purpose: The Need for Nuanced Thinking About Complex Issues

Around the same time that Toffler was writing *Future Shock*, economist Milton Friedman drew attention by declaring that "the social responsibility of business is to increase its profits." As he wrote in a widely quoted 1970 essay: "What does it mean to say that the corporate executive has a 'social responsibility' in his capacity as businessman? If this statement is not pure rhetoric, it must mean that he is to act in some way that is not in the interest of his employers."[15] Friedman even argued that spending company funds to reduce pollution beyond what was legally required violated an executive's responsibility.

While today's business leaders still show as much ambition as their predecessors—both for their organization's profitability and for their personal career advancement—they now also face a strong cross-pressure to take positions on topics that are beyond the profits and losses of their company. Many public-facing statements by corporate CEOs now include topics that go beyond making money, and that reflect the need to be accountable to a broad range of stakeholders rather than just their stockholders. Over the last several years most corporate PR teams announced with fanfare various initiatives in philanthropy, environmentalism, workforce diversity, political activism, and other spheres that contradict Friedman's thesis. (To what extent such initiatives are deeply and sincerely felt, rather than designed as virtue signaling, is a question for the next chapter.)

And yet, with the rise of social media and changes to the way media outlets cover business and political leaders, there are also strong countervailing incentives to engage in bombastic and controversial behaviors. Outlandish comments that are easily liked and shared spread far more rapidly and widely than measured, thoughtful statements. Traditionalists have complained for decades about the dominance of soundbites on television news, but the modern-day speed and viral spread of extreme or simplistic positions now makes the concerns raised by old TV shows like *Crossfire* seem quaint.

Serious leadership requires nuanced thinking about your organization's role in society as well as your personal purpose—especially in moments when working toward the public good, or even the long-term health of your organization, collides with your personal ambitions. The most important decisions you will face will rarely be black-and-white binaries between seeking or sacrificing your own rewards. That's why I like Stanford professor William Damon's definition: "Purpose is an active commitment to accomplish aims that are both meaningful to the self and of consequence to the world beyond the self."[16]

Consider Jim Fish, CEO of Waste Management, North America's leading provider of trash collection and recycling services, which has more than 20 million residential, commercial, industrial, and municipal customers. Over the past decade he has transformed the company by skillfully reconciling two pressures: the need to grow revenue and profits and the need to recycle more of the material they collect, in order to reduce the company's impact on the environment. Fish is equally committed to both sides of Waste Management's purpose, as we'll see in chapter 8, but that doesn't make it easy to balance them. And, like a true statesman, he's also deeply concerned about how to leave his company well positioned for the distant future, long after his own career has ended.

Coming Up

Of course, not every leader these days responds with statesmanship, nuance, empathy, and gravitas to the cross-pressures we've been exploring. On the contrary, many have been responding in ways that are counterproductive or even destructive to their organizations and careers, as we'll see in the next chapter.

Questions to Ponder

- Do you agree with *The Guardian* that we're living in an "age of perpetual crisis," or does that feel like an exaggeration?

- On balance, do you think leading organizations is harder or easier now, compared to several decades ago?

- Think about situations in your own career when you felt pressured to pursue two or more conflicting goals at the same time. How did you resolve those dilemmas?

- Do you think most leaders these days focus too much on improving the personal satisfaction of their people, or too little?

- Do you believe that you're primarily an inside or outside leader? How much does being forced into the opposite role take you out of your comfort zone?

- Does leading a truly global organization sound more like an exciting opportunity or a daunting challenge?

CHAPTER 2

Unserious Behaviors in a Serious World

Battle of the Billionaires

During the summer of 2023, while most business leaders were focused on the impact of inflation, the AI revolution, the war in Ukraine, and similarly weighty issues, two of the world's most prominent and powerful CEOs were threatening to beat each other up in a cage match.

Elon Musk, who had acquired Twitter the previous fall, started taunting Meta CEO Mark Zuckerberg over reports that Meta was working on a new platform to compete with Twitter, which Musk subsequently rebranded as X. Upon learning that Zuckerberg had been training in mixed martial arts and Brazilian jiujitsu, Musk challenged him to an MMA-style cage fight. Zuckerberg accepted, and negotiations began over the date, place, and conditions. The president of the Ultimate Fighting Championship (UFC) got involved in the so-called battle of the billionaires, which dominated chatter across social and mainstream media.

One might argue that Musk v. Zuck (which never actually came to pass, at least as of this writing) was just some harmless fun between competing CEOs. But during the months that they engaged in mutual taunts and threats, the social media industry faced challenges that could have risen to existential crises. Watchdogs were sounding the alarm about the ongoing rampant spread of misinformation, the rise of AI-generated fake content, and new studies about the mental health impact of social media use on children. X was also in financial trouble, as Musk's operational changes and reinstatement of controversial figures in the name of free speech drove away some users and advertisers.

In light of these business challenges, didn't both men have more important things to do than stage a cage fight? As *Wall Street Journal* columnist Daniel Henninger observed: "Mr. Zuckerberg has spent hours testifying before Congress that he is a serious person whose companies pose no threat to the psychological formation of the nation's young people. Yet here are Mr. Zuckerberg and Mr. Musk, willing to use the standing they have achieved in the U.S. business community to turn themselves into clickbait. . . . Assuming they don't fake the fight, it will be an embarrassing display of two prominent grown men in shorts rolling on the floor, pawing at each other's flesh."[1]

The Age of Unseriousness

This episode was just one highly visible and extreme example of a larger trend: the rise of unserious behavior among leaders—even extremely intelligent, talented, and successful leaders. If two of the wealthiest and most powerful CEOs in the world could get away with acting like angry teenagers, imagine the ripple effect of their influence on everyone else. While neither of them lost their jobs or fortunes, their selfishness and disregard for norms set a noxious example for their many fans. In 2023 alone, for instance, *Bloomberg News* cataloged a series of peculiar incidents involving CEOs, including the following:

- Tony Fernandes, cofounder of AirAsia, released a photo of himself shirtless and receiving a massage during a work meeting.

- Bernard Looney, CEO of BP, had to resign due to incomplete disclosures of past personal relationships with colleagues.

- Scott Kirby, United Airlines' CEO, drew criticism when it emerged that he was traveling via private jet during the airline's flight cancellation crisis.

- Greg Becker, Silicon Valley Bank's former CEO, refused to give up any part of his $10 million pay after the bank collapsed on his watch.[2]

Whether out of hubris or ignorance, many leaders are failing to truly confront the cross-pressures we just explored in chapter 1. Instead they fall back on a range of unserious behaviors that are ineffective at best, or outright destructive to their organizations and careers at worst. Let's take a closer look at the traits of these "anti–System Leader behaviors" before exploring further how an embrace of Systems Leadership can be a bulwark against both cross-pressures and the bad leadership habits they can provoke.

I see six behavioral patterns that may feel tempting to leaders in the short run but are counterproductive or even self-destructive in the longer run:

- Replacing decorum with outrageousness

- Focusing on trivial goals

- Ignoring changes you don't like

- Acting with disdain for customers

- Indulging in self-righteousness

- Failing to show spine when necessary

The common thread is that they all feel good in the moment, like eating ice cream and candy for dinner. The consequences—stomachaches and crashing from the sugar high—usually follow later.

Bad behavior may be tempting, but leaders who indulge in it sometimes overlook how transparent and public every action and statement can become these days, compared to decades past. Leaders could say and do things in the pre-internet era that would have appalled their employees and customers, but they were unlikely to be exposed publicly. These days nothing you say or do is truly private. If you call your employees lazy or your customers dumb during a group meeting or group text, your words are likely to start rocketing around social media within twenty-four hours.

Replacing Decorum with Outrageousness

The old, rigid rules of business decorum have gotten much more relaxed, in every respect from dress codes to restrictions against public swearing to the norm that leaders shouldn't vent or rant or issue ad hominem attacks. Some of these new freedoms represent progress; I certainly don't miss wearing a tie every day, and I have no problem with the occasional F-word during a meeting when used in certain contexts and geographies. The casual culture of many startups has proven that people can build extraordinary businesses far from the hushed hallways of traditional corporate offices. But things can easily get out of hand when leaders feel free or even incentivized to act outrageously in their public-facing activities, such as yelling at stock analysts during investor calls or firing off angry tweets at their perceived enemies.

It's no mystery why such outbursts are more frequent now: they deliver immediate rewards. They draw intense media attention, boost social media follower counts, intimidate opponents, and build one's reputation as a badass who can't be trifled with. It's hard to resist those temptations once you find that outrageous behavior can be an express lane to fame and influence.

Donald Trump accelerated this trend during his 2016 presidential campaign, proving that acting outrageously was a highly effective way to capture and hold the spotlight. Why bother creating and announcing a detailed economic or healthcare plan, which would take a huge amount of work? Trump showed that it was far easier to dominate a news cycle with taunts and insults. Seeing Trump's success with capturing the spotlight, politicians on both sides of the aisle began to emulate his attention-grabbing outrageousness. For instance, Congresswoman Alexandria Ocasio-Cortez (D-New York) taunted her critics by tweeting, "If Republicans are mad they can't date me they can just say that instead of projecting their sexual frustrations."[3] She quickly became one of the most prominent American politicians of her generation.

Another kind of outrageousness helped Sam Bankman-Fried, the now-convicted founder of the defunct crypto exchange FTX, who played up his awkward-nerd-genius persona and disregard for traditional business practices. He showed up for video calls with venture capitalists looking completely disheveled and would frequently look off camera during such meetings to play video games on another screen. Instead of being horrified and driven away by such disrespect, numerous VCs took Bankman-Fried's behavior as a green flag. The less he seemed to care what they thought of him, the more confidence he projected and the more brilliant and innovative investors assumed he must have been. He provoked a frenzy among investors who wanted a seat on the FTX rocket ship before it blasted off for the moon.

And here's another Musk example—not because I have any bias against him but because he's such a high-profile role model. During a public Q&A session in November 2023, journalist Andrew Ross Sorkin asked him about the trend of advertisers pulling their budgets from X. Musk's "free-speech absolutist" policies were re-platforming some extreme voices, including some who spread conspiracy theories against people of color, Jews, and the LGBTQ community. Sorkin identified Disney CEO Bob Iger as one of those reluctant to advertise on the new version of X, and Musk shot back in anger: "Don't advertise! If someone is going to try and blackmail me with advertising? Blackmail me with money? Go f— yourself! Go f— yourself, is that clear? Hey Bob, if you're in the audience, that's how I feel. Don't advertise."[4]

Not surprisingly, the richest man in the world telling the CEO of The Walt Disney Company to go f— himself dominated the headlines and social media. In fact, it drowned out coverage of everything else said at that conference, not merely by Musk but by every other attendee. His fans cheered, while his detractors (and, I assume, some of his coinvestors in X) were horrified. That public outburst may have felt good, but it further risked X's advertising revenue by confirming Musk's volatility and lack of respect for his customers. A serious leader would have been diplomatic in public, while setting up a private conversation with Iger to try to resolve their conflict out of the spotlight.

This is not to say that outrageous behavior or statements are always inappropriate. Richard Branson has spent decades promoting the Virgin Group through headline-drawing stunts, such as attempting to circumnavigate the globe in a hot air balloon. The key distinction is that every provocative action or statement from Branson was calculated to build Virgin Group's brand and draw positive attention to its businesses and products. He got people talking without indulging in personal attacks on his competitors, partners, or customers.

A simple rule of thumb: How would you feel if your child engaged in a certain kind of behavior at school or among their peers? If words or deeds are too outrageous for a middle-schooler, they are probably not worthy of a serious business leader.

Focusing on Trivial Goals

Another type of unserious behavior that's been trending for more than a decade is pursuing objectives that ultimately don't matter much, though they may be interesting or profitable in the short run.

One of the mantras of Systems Leadership is "Solve problems that matter." I remind my students and clients that the world is full of hard problems whose solutions can benefit the greater good, while simultaneously driving a company's growth and profitability. Ideally, our brightest leaders and technologists would focus their talents and energies on improving outcomes and reducing costs in healthcare, finding cleaner and more capital efficient ways to generate energy for 8 billion humans, or improving supply chains before the next global pandemic arrives. One of my favorite Systems Leaders is Naomi Allen, cofounder and CEO of Brightline, which uses technology to improve behavioral health support for children and their families.

But, at least from my perspective in Silicon Valley, it seems like many of the best young minds of the past decade focused on goals such as becoming influencers, creating yet another food delivery app, or (arguably worse) marketing NFTs or crypto tokens.

I don't wish to denigrate everyone who pursues a career in entertainment, social media, or lifestyle services and products. Such fields can create true value and pleasure for millions of customers. And sometimes the well-intentioned pursuit of innovations that have the potential to improve the world ultimately fail, such as the Google Glass smart glasses of a decade ago. But some would-be innovations deserve our skepticism. NFTs lacked utility from day one, at least relative to their hype. Beware the danger of chasing any "Emperor's New Clothes" trend just because lots of other smart people are doing the same thing.

Ignoring Changes You Don't Like

This pitfall is exceptionally common: Continuing to act as if your industry or your job function hasn't fundamentally changed in the past five, ten, or even twenty years. Telling yourself that disruptive technologies or business models are merely fads that can be safely ignored until they pass. Hoping that the traditional ways of the universe will somehow reassert themselves. There are countless examples, ranging from downplaying the potential impact of generative AI or the shift to clean energy to assuming that as Gen Z workers age they will naturally embrace the culture and practices of their elders.

Consider something as basic as workplace communication technology. Boomers in corporate America grew up with typed and carbon copied interoffice memos and made lots of spontaneous phone calls. If you had a question for a colleague, you were expected to pick up the phone. Generation X then led the way during the email revolution of the 1990s, often to the frustration of elders who would rather call than email. Then the Millennials embraced texting, especially after everyone began carrying a smartphone 24/7. Now Gen Z's communications are increasingly centered on platforms like Slack, which are often more effective than email for asking questions to groups, posting announcements, and managing collaborative schedules.

You may personally hate Slack, but your personal preferences don't matter much. If you work in a Slack-driven culture, your only options are getting good at Slack or accepting obsolescence.

If you are over forty, let me ask you this: Do you have the TikTok app on your phone, and do you check it from time to time? Have you experimented with ChatGPT or other generative AI engines for an actual work problem or assignment? Have you used WhatsApp for international communication? You might think some of the above are overhyped or no better than existing solutions, but how can you be sure without taking them for a test drive? And how will you relate to employees who view you as an old person yelling at clouds?[5]

Similarly, the remote work practices that COVID made necessary became popular with white-collar employees, many of whom lobbied to keep working from home after the pandemic began to subside. Many argued that they were actually *more* productive when they didn't have to waste time commuting or fending off frequent interruptions in an open-plan workspace. Some studies (including one by economists at the Federal Reserve Bank of San Francisco) backed them up, finding that remote work generally didn't hurt productivity or other key metrics.[6] And 2024 research by Stanford economist Nicholas Bloom concluded that hybrid work was often the best model; employees who worked from home two days a week were just as productive and just as likely to be promoted as their fully office-based peers, and were significantly less likely to quit.[7] Despite this evidence, many leaders continued to push assertively or even aggressively for strict in-office policies—and this has been increasing as I write this. Some have chosen not to accept a new world where people might come into the office just two or three days per week, or even two or three days per year.

Finally, have you considered what role luck and timing have played in your personal success, or that of your company? Leaders need self-awareness to recognize when they've benefited sharply from catching the right trend at the right time—a trend that, by definition, can't last forever. Was your company offering exactly the kind of product investors were looking for, just when they were flush with cash? Were you able to lock in long-term financing at a moment when interest rates seemed permanently frozen near zero? Fully understanding the reasons for past successes can help you internalize whether your old "playbook" is still useful for a current or future challenge.

Acting with Disdain for Customers

Let me stress that showing what I call "disdain" for customers is different from failing to fully satisfy them (which can follow a sincere but inadequate effort) or trying to maximize profit by charging whatever your market can bear. Instead, I define disdain as exploiting, abusing, neglecting, or taking unfair advantage of customers, whether or not any laws are broken in the process. Disdain can even be accidental, if such treatment is the unintended consequence of poorly chosen policies.

Leaders at all levels role-model either respect, disdain, or something in between, and their attitude is contagious. When customers become annoying, frustrating, or unreasonable in their demands, it's tempting to disparage them. Your team will absorb your mindset and act accordingly, perhaps treating customers with spite or indifference.

Consider Apple's longstanding refusal to provide seamless integrated access to its iMessage app to include smartphones that use the Android operating system. This is why texts sent between iPhone and Android users show up with a green SMS bubble instead of iMessage's branded blue bubble—even if a group chat includes a dozen iPhone users and only one Android user. This has turned the green bubble into a marker of second-class status, particularly in the United States, from middle schools to college campuses to workplaces. "On dating apps, green-bubble users are often rejected by the blues. Adults with iPhones have been known to privately snicker to one another when a green bubble taints a group chat. In schools, a green bubble is an invitation for mockery and exclusion by children with iPhones, according to Common Sense Media, a nonprofit that focuses on technology's impact on families."[8]

This isn't just a matter of social stigma; many emojis and animations fail to transmit across the blue-green divide, and pictures and videos tend to be delivered more slowly and with reduced quality. It would have been trivially easy for Apple engineers to make texts frictionless between iMessage and other popular texting protocols like RCS, thus benefiting both iPhone and Android users. The fact that they didn't can only mean that Apple intentionally and disdainfully delivered a worse experience both to its own customers and to potential future customers (including me, as a longtime buyer of Apple computers and other products who nevertheless prefers the Google Pixel smartphone).

We know that the peer pressure created by the stigma and friction of green bubbles works to Apple's advantage. Some unknowable number of customers switch to an iPhone every year because they're tired of being criticized or mocked. CEO Tim Cook has denied that this was Apple's reason for restricting access to iMessage, claiming instead that his customers hadn't requested it. But I know I've requested it, as have other Apple customers, and in return we got little but disdain and excuses. Apple only recently made adjustments to this situation because they were forced to do so by European regulators—not because they really care about what their customers want.

Here's an example from a local business whose disdain stung me even more personally. I subscribed digitally to my local newspaper, the *San Jose Mercury News,* for a dozen years and cared about its survival. Then in 2023, it raised my monthly rate for a digital subscription from $14 to $22. That seemed steep, but I shrugged it off because inflation was high and good journalism is expensive to produce. But then I noticed that the paper's website still offered new subscribers a $14 monthly plan. When I called to ask why current readers were hit with a 50 percent increase while newcomers could still get the old rate, customer service gave me a runaround for about forty-five minutes. First, they offered me an $11 one-time credit. Then they said I could renew for $18 per month. When I asked why I shouldn't just cancel and sign up again for $14, I was put on hold for ten minutes. The rep finally came back and begrudgingly offered me $14. But at that point I was so fed up that I canceled instead. The paper had crossed the line from bad customer service into full-blown disdain.

Indulging in Self-Righteousness

This type of unserious behavior might be framed as the opposite of outrageousness. Many leaders are tempted to speak out self-righteously on controversial public issues or to engage in demonstrative gestures, with the primary goal of looking good to their peers and the media. Making a statement on the company's social media accounts—such as denouncing police violence or giving their perspective on laws in other parts of the world—can make leaders feel good about their own moral virtue.

The problem is that few issues are truly unambiguous, and culture war controversies in particular inflame passions on all sides. Indulging in self-righteousness on nuanced subjects unrelated (or even tangentially related) to your business can easily backfire. If you send a message that you don't want to work with or do business with people who disagree with you, that can profoundly alienate customers or employees.

During a tense moment in the 2016 presidential campaign, the partners of the venture capital firm CRV released a statement with the provocative all-caps title "F**K TRUMP." They argued that "Donald Trump's anti-immigration statements are diametrically opposed to the core values of entrepreneurship. And at CRV, we've had enough. The CRV partnership—united and unanimous—rejects Donald Trump's candidacy for President of the United States."[9] They went on to make a passionate case for defending "immigrants, the sons and daughters of immigrants, and anyone with the immigrant spirit."[10] They also announced that CRV would cover the costs of U.S. visas for any startup founders they funded, and would create a fellowship program to support other immigrant entrepreneurs.

I agreed with their position on immigration and admired their initiatives. But I was struck by their use of self-righteous clickbait. The headline was needlessly inflammatory, and so was this conclusion: "If you are for building walls and stopping change, stay away. Bigots need not apply."[11] This strongly implied that CRV would automatically reject any entrepreneurs who voted for Trump. To me, at least, that wasn't a noble stance; it was the embodiment of smug, pompous, liberal elitism. It told me that defending immigrants was actually less important to CRV than looking cool and progressive to their fellow VCs and startup founders.

Not surprisingly, given the power of calculated outrageousness, this piece was shared all over Silicon Valley and drew a ton of clicks and comments. It raised the profile of CRV far more than a less aggressive piece with a serious title, perhaps one like "Immigration Is the Foundation upon Which Our Country Is Built." If drawing attention was their primary goal, they succeeded.

Now let's consider how businesses deal with another highly polarizing and emotional issue. I'm friends with a woman I'll call Jane, who graduated from the Stanford GSB two decades ago and now leads a healthcare startup. When the Supreme Court overturned *Roe v. Wade* in 2022, allowing conservative states to ban abortion, she was under a lot of pressure from her staff to issue a statement of protest. Jane also felt strongly about the topic, and she believed it would impact her company's future business. So she wrote an opinion piece for a prominent media outlet, expressing her disagreement at this curtailment of women's rights and how it would threaten women's lives.

A few days later, Jane got an email from one of her female employees, saying that she loved the company but now felt obligated to resign. This woman was pro-life and felt that she was clearly not welcome at the company because of her beliefs. Despite a respectful exchange, Jane was unable to convince the woman to stay. Jane then shared the email with her DEI team, who responded to the effect that this was no great loss—that the company was better off without someone who didn't support their pro-choice values. But Jane remained upset and self-critical—and realized that she needed to change how her company looked at DEI. One of her core values was making all of her people feel valued and included, but she and the company had failed to live up to their stated value of inclusion, and she had not met her own personal standard of leadership.

The world is complicated and human beings are complicated, and sometimes two or more of your values will come into conflict. Be wary of the temptation to divide everyone into good people and bad people, or to treat nuanced issues as having binary answers— right or wrong, you're either with us or against us.

Even the question of doing business with partners based in dictatorships can be nuanced. Mathias Döpfner, CEO of Axel Springer, wrote an entire book to wrestle with the conundrum of whether and how to do business ethically in authoritarian countries. I confronted this issue myself in Saudi Arabia, which I first visited with a group of students in 2017. Over subsequent years I developed relationships with many people there, in both the Saudi government and the private sector. When I was invited to do some consulting and teaching there, I wondered if I should accept the invitation. This was around the time that many Americans were protesting Saudi Arabia's highly repressive policies toward some members of society and its treatment of many residents as second-class citizens.

However, after learning much more about Saudi Arabia's history and people, I decided that I could have a more positive impact by engaging with this country of 36 million, even if I disagreed with some of its government's values and behaviors. Someone else might have made a principled decision to decline these opportunities. But I felt that no benefit would come from my grandstanding over a public boycott, whereas my presence in Saudi Arabia might have some influence on the people I worked with there. The people I met also greatly influenced me with their energy, kindness, and intelligence.

Failing to Show Spine when Necessary

As self-critical leaders seek to stamp out unhelpful bouts of self-righteousness, they'll likely conclude that some issues do require taking a principled stance even if it upsets some of your allies, customers, or employees. Some standards need to be upheld to preserve credibility and legitimacy for the long run, even if doing so leads to short-term pain. When leaders can't resist the temptation to give in to inappropriate demands, or when they put their heads in the sand rather than showing spine, they usually come to regret it.

A tragic example became widespread in the fall of 2023, when a vicious terrorist attack by Hamas provoked Israel into a retaliatory war against Hamas in Gaza. Thousands of civilians were killed in both Israel and Gaza, provoking intense global debates about which side was more to blame for all that death and destruction. On American college campuses, these debates often escalated into shockingly aggressive antisemitic protests, not merely against the Israeli government but against the global Jewish community, and some protestors called for the outright destruction of Israel. Unfortunately, this sometimes led to counter-incidents that became hateful toward all Palestinians and their supporters, not merely toward Hamas, making campuses toxic for multiple groups.

I'm sure that being a university president during such turmoil was not pleasant. But those high-profile campus conflicts gave leaders in higher education an opportunity—and an obligation—to stand up for a sharp distinction between free speech and hate speech. It was time for them to say something like this, clearly and firmly: "Our university supports open and respectful debate on public policy issues, but not ad hominem attacks on individuals or groups, no matter who they are. While hate speech might be protected by the law, if you can't understand or accept that distinction, you don't align with our values. That's not who we are and not what we expect in our community."

Very few university presidents, alas, displayed the spine necessary to draw that type of line in the sand and risk a revolt among particular groups. The presidents of Harvard and the University of Pennsylvania even lost their jobs after equivocating at a congressional hearing about whether a hypothetical student's call for genocide against Jews would violate their codes of conduct.

Twenty Years and Five Minutes

Pointing out unserious behavior isn't the same as passing a sweeping judgment on a leader's character. We're all human, and we all give in to different kinds of temptation, at least sometimes. But that never means we're incapable of learning and growing.

In my case, my biggest leadership vice was indulging my impulse toward righteous rage. In my twenties and thirties, whenever I confronted someone else's stupid mistakes (or at least what seemed like stupid mistakes to me), I'd fire off angry "flame emails." Those emails were eloquent, passionate, well organized, and packed with irrefutable facts and sublime insults. I became a master at writing them. There was just one problem: those angry emails *always* failed to achieve my goals. They felt cathartic to write and send, but giving myself that burst of adrenaline inevitably made the situation worse. I would have to spend days cleaning up my own messes.

Sadly, it took many years before I learned to resist that temptation. Nowadays I sometimes still get angry at stupid mistakes. I sometimes still write harsh emails. But now I try to keep those emails permanently in a drafts folder, where they can't do any damage to my professional relationships. I'm not perfect, but I'm working to improve. So I know how hard it can be to model serious behavior for your team, especially when so many political and business leaders constantly model unserious behavior.

No business school can overcome the surrounding culture its

students grow up with or the tactics they're exposed to daily—tactics that have been undeniably effective for many public figures. Even if some leaders get away with more than seems reasonable, most of us mere mortals will not be as fortunate if we copy their antics. And, while we can't assume that unserious leaders will ever fall from their perches of wealth and power, we can wonder how their long-term legacies will be viewed. If you care about what your colleagues will say about you in five, ten, or thirty years, that's reason enough to take leadership seriously and treat your responsibilities with the gravitas they deserve. I haven't worked for the late Andy Grove since 1998, but I still think often about the inspiring example he set for results-oriented yet empathic leadership, especially during times of high stress and adversity.

Warren Buffett once said, "It takes twenty years to build a reputation and five minutes to ruin it. If you think about that, you'll do things differently."[12] Unserious behavior might win you some tactical advantages in the short run or even in the medium run. But in the long run it will undermine your career, your team, your company, and especially your reputation. If you can avoid it, you will win friends and admirers for life.

Coming Up

At this point I won't blame you if you're feeling a little discouraged. From the vantage point of the intense challenges and cross-pressures we've been exploring, leadership roles might not seem very appealing at all! Starting with chapter 3, fortunately, our examples will become much more inspiring.

The people I call Systems Leaders, at companies large and small in a wide range of industries, understand Buffett's point deep in their bones, and therefore do things very differently indeed. You will soon see how skillfully they navigate these cross-pressures, while avoiding or at least minimizing the setbacks that have befallen many of their peers. These Systems Leaders achieve successful results for their organizations while serving as role models for those around them. The next chapter offers an overview of their mindsets, strategies, and tactics.

Questions to Ponder

- What unserious behaviors do you see in your company or industry? How are those behaviors treated by others?

- What changes are you or your company ignoring that you don't like? Why are you and/or the company ignoring them?

- How do you react when you encounter behavior that seems self-righteous rather than genuine? Where do you see that kind of behavior most often? What do you do to prevent yourself from falling into the same temptation?

- Where do you see disdain for customers in your industry? What would you change about your industry to reduce any symptoms of disdain?

CHAPTER 3

A Better Alternative: Systems Leadership

The Urgency of Systems Leadership

So, what is "Systems Leadership"—and what am I really getting at with that first word, *systems*? I define it as the ability to master processes and strategies from different perspectives at the same time: physical and digital, breadth of market and depth of market, short term and long term, what's good for the company and what's good for its ecosystem. Systems Leaders combine the IQ to understand their company's technology and business model with the EQ to build effective teams and inspire them to new heights. They use short-term execution skills to hit their financial targets this year, while also driving changes that may not pay off for five or more years. They grasp the big picture and essential details simultaneously. They understand how all the elements of an organization affect both internal and external stakeholders, and how interactions internally and externally shape a company's outcomes.

When I described Systems Leadership to one Fortune 500 CEO, his response was "Wow, that sounds hard." He was right, of course. But Systems Leadership is hard in the same sense that running a marathon, playing guitar, doing calculus, or driving on a highway are hard. For all of those competencies, the baseline of required innate talents isn't very rare. The key is putting in consistent effort over time to learn and then master the necessary skills. It's about practice much more than talent.

If you're reading this, I have no doubt that you have the intellectual and emotional right stuff to become a Systems Leader. I have seen these strategies and tactics work for department heads and mid-level executives in all kinds of organizations, including many who don't have business degrees or other advanced education. Time and again, I've seen these ideas land powerfully with my executive education and corporate lecture audiences, many of whom report back on how helpful it is to think and act like a Systems Leader.

If you choose to commit to this goal, it can make a massive difference to your career. Systems Leadership might determine whether you'll rise as far as your talents can take you or whether you'll get stuck along the way. It can even determine your entire organization's success or failure, whether you work for a large incumbent or a small upstart. The stakes really are that high.

The Origins of Systems Leadership

Jeff Immelt and I began to develop Systems Leadership in 2017, just before his retirement as CEO of GE. We met to explore the possibility of teaching a class together at the Stanford GSB so he could

impart some of what he'd learned the hard way to the next generation. I was very interested to partner with a leader who had been
through so much—a leader who had experienced both the highest
highs and some of the lowest lows possible in the corporate world.
It was telling that he titled his memoir *Hot Seat: What I Learned
Leading a Great American Company.*

Beginning with our first discussion, Jeff and I discovered a
shared concern. We both felt that the typical business school
curriculum—even at a top-tier institution like Stanford—had crucial gaps when it came to addressing the unique challenges of our
time. We agreed, of course, that aspiring business leaders still need
to learn finance, strategy, operations, marketing, and other traditional subjects. They still need a firm grasp of pricing models and
the weighted average cost of capital, plus softer skills such as motivating and coaching their people. But all those isolated skills were
no longer enough. Even the most acclaimed and cutting-edge business schools, which stressed the importance of both IQ and EQ,
weren't fully preparing students for the cross-pressures they would
face in the real world.

The response to the first iteration of our new course was very
positive, and we kept refining it. When COVID hit in the spring
of 2020, during our third year of teaching the course, we realized
that Systems Leadership dovetails with crisis leadership. Many of
the guest speakers who joined us remotely that quarter described
confronting challenges they had never even imagined and for
which they had no playbook. For instance, Ryan Lance, CEO of
the giant energy company ConocoPhillips, spoke to our students
on the day that the price of crude oil turned *negative,* due to the
pandemic-driven shock to the global economy. How do you deal
with a problem so unprecedented that it's hard even to conceptu-
alize it?

COVID was an especially good example of how leaders can confront extreme, sudden disruption without losing their bearings, their confidence, or the respect of their people. The pandemic became a teachable crisis to evolve our framework and tools for responding to truly unpredictable disruptions. We wanted to prepare our students, whether they faced such shocks soon after graduation or decades in the future.

Systems Leaders Are Better Prepared for Higher Expectations

For much of the last two hundred years, the leaders of huge companies have played prominent roles in both society and politics. One need only to think of titans such as John D. Rockefeller, Henry Ford, J. P. Morgan, and Andrew Carnegie in the nineteenth and early twentieth centuries, or Steve Jobs, Bill Gates, Jeff Bezos, and Elon Musk in the late twentieth and twenty-first centuries, to appreciate the impact these people have had beyond the companies they built.

But, over the past two decades, *every* leader in business has been asked to confront the kind of issues that were once reserved only for the prominent men and women who ran very large companies. In a world where every product and service is connected, even small companies are crossing international borders and dealing with issues navigating cultural and national interests in ways that firms of their size did not have to consider previously.

Take, for example, the great power conflict between the United States and China. Whether one is dealing with supply chain complexities, data protection, or (if one is outside both superpowers) which technical stack should be chosen for product development, today's leaders need to understand how their choices will impact their suppliers, their customers, and their employees. In addition, leaders are required to work with governments not just by lobbying for certain policies, or to keep ahead of regulatory changes, but also to ensure that governments are aware of the challenges facing private enterprise. Issues such as cybersecurity have come to the forefront for every organization, as attacks on companies' IT infrastructure are carried out by state actors against commercial institutions. The old wish that governments would simply "leave business alone" has become impractical in a hyperconnected world. Like it or not, leaders now need to learn how to engage with government mindsets.

Meanwhile, they are also forced to deal with cultural changes that have raised the bar on expectations. For instance, employees now want to know where their leaders stand on social issues, many of which are highly charged and controversial, requiring delicate nuance. Business executives are also increasingly asked to be good stewards and leaders not just for their shareholders, but of their communities, their countries, and society at large. One could argue that this situation has been exacerbated by the decline in stature of other traditional institutions that used to take on these roles (e.g., governments, religious organizations, families, etc.), but it is unambiguous that most business leaders have not been trained in, nor had the time to think deeply about, many of the complex issues they are asked to publicly address—often on short notice and during volatile moments.

Even complexities around the future of work are challenging leaders to develop and implement policies on remote and hybrid work, and to consider the unintended consequences of how these choices might impact a company and its people. And with the continued advancement of technologies such as artificial intelligence, machine learning, robotics, and autonomous systems, leaders need to think constantly about retraining their labor forces. If they assume that employees will acquire new skills on their own initiative in their spare time, it's easy to be left with an underprepared, subpar team.

Systems Leadership Begins with Appreciating Multiple Perspectives

Traditionally, executives rose to senior management through expertise in one particular function, such as operations, engineering, sales, marketing, or finance. When put in charge of a business unit or a whole company, their backgrounds naturally biased them toward seeing the landscape through one primary perspective. To cover everything else, they tended to rely heavily on colleagues who were experts in other functions, including R&D, human resources, legal, and government relations. Leaders could set broad goals, delegate the details, and assume that things would work out, as long as they had a competent team. There was no need to be immersed in every department's details.

But the complexity of modern business makes that dynamic outdated, with every function more interdependent than ever. For instance, a small shift in the sales department's strategy can now wreak havoc on manufacturing and finance, and vice versa. And every player in a company's external ecosystem of partners, competitors, and customers can shake up carefully laid plans at any moment. As a result, today's leaders need to be good at fitting *all* these pieces together to deliver optimal value to customers and shareholders.

This is not to imply that they need to be omniscient or memorize every detail of every aspect of their business. No one can possibly do that. But Systems Leaders learn enough to have meaningful conversations with experts of all stripes. (This relates to the product manager's mindset, which we'll return to shortly.) They learn how to ask the right questions, not necessarily how to answer all of them. Then they evaluate how the perspectives of those experts fit into the bigger picture of the company's strategic priorities, as well as those of its ecosystem partners. Then, finally, they muster the self-confidence and courage to make decisions under extreme uncertainty.

To develop this required breadth of knowledge, Systems Leaders commit to lifelong learning and remain open to new experiences. This might include anything from taking courses on artificial intelligence to buying coffee for entry-level colleagues and researching how additive manufacturing is changing where factories should be built. Above all, it means breaking out of information bubbles—resisting the urge to stick exclusively with people from the same background, who all see the world the same way.

A Third Way of Leadership

For the past few decades, leadership models have often been described in binary terms, with an alleged schism between the traditional, hierarchical, slow-moving corporate world and the more nimble, risk-taking, and disruptive leadership style of the startup world. That binary is oversimplified, of course, but it's still instructive to compare the stereotypical attributes of traditional leaders, Silicon Valley–style leaders, and a third way exemplified by Systems Leaders. This table looks at the attitudes of these three groups with regard to six major aspects of leading an organization or business unit:

Their preferred . . .	Incumbent Leader	Disruptive Leader	Systems Leader
Markets	Vertical (domain)	Horizontal (platform)	Scalable on both axes
Technology	Hardware (assets)	Software (platform)	Innovative platform with an operating front end
Outcomes	Continuous improvement	Winner takes all	Dominant share
Workers	Long-term / loyal	Flexible / gig	Portfolio career
Customers	"Units of one"	Single platform	"Customizable off the shelf"
Government	Hands-on and regulator	Libertarian	Balanced

Incumbent leaders at companies that are already successful tend to focus on vertical markets—building great products for a narrow but deep pool of potential customers. Vertical success is often hardware based, and outcomes are often framed around continuous improvement. Think of BMW making its cars just a little more fuel efficient and advanced every year. Or think of Burger King considering it a win if its revenue grows just a percentage point or two more than McDonald's or Wendy's in a given year. Incumbent leaders try to inspire employees to stay with an organization for many years to reap the benefits of institutional memory. They think about customers as "units of one" who prefer customized, distinctive solutions that will generate lock-in, or at least strong brand loyalty. And they see nothing wrong with hands-on government regulation of their industry, because they probably have enough clout to turn government relations (i.e., lobbying) into a competitive advantage by keeping out competition.

Disruptive leaders are more likely to be obsessed with building a horizontal platform that can scale to infinity. For instance, Meta won't be satisfied until every human on the planet is using at least one of their products; the first 3.5 billion users of Facebook, Instagram, and WhatsApp represent less than the halfway point. They prefer software over hardware, because it's much easier to scale than any physical product. Their ideal outcome is winner take all, because platform-driven markets tend to settle on one dominant player (such as the Google search engine and Uber for ride-sharing in the United States), due to network effects. Disruptive leaders tend to define their ideal workers as flexible—either gig based or people who willingly change jobs every year or two. Their ideal customers are happy with a single basic offering, which also makes scaling easier. And their ideal government is libertarian, imposing minimal regulations or interference.

Systems Leaders combine the best of both sets of skills and attitudes. They understand and appreciate both hardware and software, both vertical expertise and horizontal scale. They aren't hell-bent on achieving winner-take-all dominance, because they want bigger outcomes than fighting for each fraction of a point of market share. They try to build employee loyalty by delivering both financial and emotional benefits, but they understand that long tenures at a single company are increasingly rare. Their ideal customers seek a "customizable off the shelf" (COTS) solution that can easily be tweaked to individual needs. (Think of the Netflix algorithms that make a sci-fi fan's browsing experience so different from a rom-com fan's.) And Systems Leaders see the ideal government as balanced—regulating products and protecting workers where appropriate, but never overregulating in ways that inhibit innovation or hurt customers.

The Orchestra Conductor Without a Score

It helps to imagine a Systems Leader as an orchestra conductor, surrounded not only by all the functions within the company but also by external forces such as demanding customers, aggressive competitors, and unreliable ecosystem partners. Most conductors come from a background of expertise on a single instrument, and they have to widen their perspective when they move to the podium. Good conductors retune their ears to take in all the instruments at once and get them all working in harmony. Now, this metaphor isn't perfect. Conductors, after all, have a score in front of them, spelling out exactly how every instrument should be contributing to the piece. Systems Leaders, on the other hand, operate in a state of constant uncertainty about what might happen next. Instead of relying on a score, they often know only the basic tune. But they still have to inspire the team to play harmoniously together.

Systems Leaders rely on their ability to recognize patterns and apply past experiences to new situations. They combine the clarity to focus on improving the lives and fortunes of their customers with the courage to lead their people into the unknown.

Let's look at five powerful competencies that help these conductors get the best performance out of every section of the orchestra, without allowing the overall sound to collapse in cacophony. These will be recurring themes in the stories of real Systems Leaders in subsequent chapters:

- Operating at intersections

- Preparing for the future

- Managing context

- Thinking like a product manager

- Embracing risk during uncertainty and disruption

Operating at Intersections

Operating at intersections means pursuing two or more goals at the same time, because you know that succeeding at each of them will deliver powerful synergies that you couldn't get from pursuing each goal separately. There can be many types of intersections that fit this criterion. For instance:

An innovative technology meets an innovative business model. This powerful combination drives some of the most successful companies of our time. Align Technology, for example, blended cutting-edge technology (Invisalign tooth aligners, made via digital scanners and 3D printers) with an innovative business model (recruiting dentists to become a channel partner to offer orthodonture to adults). The result has been a huge success over the past two decades, with customers loving the chance to get straighter teeth via a convenient, affordable, nearly invisible process. Align might have succeeded with its new technologies alone, or with its new business model alone, but the synergy was more valuable by orders of magnitude.

Short-term results meet long-term innovation. In the old days, a company would elevate leaders who were great at running a business unit according to its plan and hitting its quarterly and annual targets. The company might also celebrate visionary thinkers who could plot new strategies for five or ten years out. But operators and innovators were treated as separate groups with very different skill sets. Today, in contrast, Systems Leaders know how to operate at scale *and* how to manage innovation. In fact, they find their greatest satisfaction at that intersection. For instance, we will soon meet Jochen Zeitz, the German-born CEO of an iconic American company, Harley-Davidson. He has skillfully led Harley's innovations in electric motorcycles (which eventually became a stand-alone company, LiveWire) without compromising the growth and profitability of its core motorcycle business.

Global strength meets local expertise. We introduced this challenge in chapter 1 with the example of Kering, which has to juggle the local priorities of its luxury brands in more than thirty-five countries, while maximizing the benefits of the stellar global reputation of those brands. Systems leaders are adept at understanding the dynamics at both levels as they do their jobs.

"What we're already good at" meets "new ways to apply these skills." It can be extremely rewarding to scan the horizon for connections between a current competitive advantage and an opportunity to apply that competency to a different field. For instance, the South Korean electronics giant Samsung realized that its world-class manufacturing process for semiconductors, which requires clean rooms, advanced equipment, and strong operational discipline, could also become a competitive advantage for manufacturing

pharmaceuticals. By extending their existing expertise to a radically different field, Samsung's leaders created a huge opportunity for growth. In fact, the company is now one of the world's largest manufacturers of generic biologic drugs.

Preparing for the Future

You don't need to be a professional futurist to predict which technologies are going to continue to impact business and society for at least the next decade, among them robotics, data analytics, artificial intelligence, machine learning, cloud computing, blockchain, and additive manufacturing. The challenge is figuring out how such innovations will affect various aspects of your organization, including core functions like administration, R&D, sales, and manufacturing. Like it or not, certain jobs in all of those areas will become obsolete, while new jobs that don't even have titles yet will be created.

These unavoidable trends force Systems Leaders to make tough decisions. They wrestle with which functions a company should handle itself, and which ones it should outsource. They build scale intelligently, staffing up or retraining employees to replace the ones whose old jobs are going away. They weigh the risks of making too many changes too quickly against the risk of being left behind their competitors.

As you make such tough decisions yourself, be mindful of the biases you've developed over your career. There's nothing shameful about being biased, as long as you're self-aware enough to recognize when you might be wrong. For instance, I was trained as a business unit operator, so I look at opportunities from an operating perspective. People who trained as engineers, accountants, sales reps, or lawyers will see the world very differently.

Another pitfall to avoid when predicting the future is group-think. One of my favorite aphorisms comes from Carl Ice, former CEO of BNSF Railway: "You're never wrong in your own conference room." Systems Leaders seek outside opinions from trusted sources beyond their direct reports. They get out of the office regularly to visit remote facilities and meet with informal advisors. Ice told my class that every year he rode at least twelve thousand miles on his railroad, so he could see firsthand the condition of its operations.[1] Anyone insightful enough to understand the industry and honest enough to challenge the leader's conclusions can become a valuable sounding board.

Managing Context

Context is commonly defined as "the set of circumstances or facts that surround a particular event, situation, etc."[2] Facts in isolation are not truth; they can lead you badly astray if you misunderstand their context. To emphasize this point, I often show my classes a slide with a simple equation that I learned from Jeff Immelt:

$$\text{Truth} = \text{Facts} + \text{Context}$$

Especially during times of great volatility, there can be broad agreement on the facts of what's happening but sharp disagreement about the context. The leader's responsibility is to define and explain context—to separate signal from noise—as situations evolve.

For instance, during the 1980s most American business leaders saw globalization as a virtually unambiguous good, a way to sell more stuff around the world while reducing supply costs and (via offshoring) labor costs. But over the last decade, while the fundamentals of global free trade have remained basically the same, the context is now very different. China has become a rising global superpower, not just a place to make sneakers or cell phones cheaply. Offshoring has devastated large parts of the industrial Midwest in the United States, contributing to the opioid crisis and populist politics, among other consequences. Even Germany, whose largest trading partner is China, is now seeing unexpected competition from Chinese companies in their traditional businesses.[3] Rather than rushing into new avenues for globalization that seem beneficial on the surface, Systems Leaders take time to consider the wider context.

Another example of managing context came up when I was teaching a case study about social media. I asked the room why Meta has become widely hated in recent years, while its fellow tech giant Google—which also tracks and monetizes the actions of its users—has avoided that kind of visceral negative reaction. My students were stumped, until a guest speaker noted that Google's declared mission is organizing the world's information to help you find whatever you want. If a Google search helps you find something, Google doesn't care whether the information lives somewhere else. Their goal is to be helpful enough that you'll want to return, not to keep you in a walled garden of content. In other words, Meta's business model is particularly great for Meta—even at the expense of the people who use their products: users get addicted to consuming and sharing content, which makes platforms like Facebook more effective for targeted advertising. But when you consider the context of user resentment and feelings of exploitation, the long-term dangers of that model become clear.

Systems Leaders think about the context of every message they share with staff, via any medium. They never forget that risk and uncertainty can scare the hell out of their people. Asking them to change the way they've been operating for years is much more effective when done with a tone of quiet determination, not panic. A context of reassurance and calm can go a long way, even if you feel the opposite of calm inside.

Explaining a decision by saying, "We have to make this change for these reasons, we know how to do it, let's get started," is a powerful way to drive change. Command-and-control leadership is much less effective than it used to be; talented people want to know the *why* behind every *what*. If a leader treats them like adults who can acknowledge and accept trade-offs and uncertainties, people will be inclined to trust that leader's well-considered path toward a destination that feels appropriate.

Even the famously tough and confrontational Nick Saban, former head football coach of the University of Alabama, adjusted his leadership style in the last few years of his iconic career. He learned to resist the temptation to boss his players around from a top-down perspective, with the unspoken subtext that *"You need to do X because I told you to"* or even *"Do X because it's in the best interests of the team."* Instead, Saban began to take extra time to explain why X would support a player's own best interests. As one football analyst observed, "Saban's evolution wasn't born out of compassion, but of self-interest. Today's players are different, no longer willing to do what they're told simply because it's what they were told. They want to know why."[4]

Thinking Like a Product Manager

In many companies, the product manager is at the hub of a wheel-shaped org chart, constantly interacting with engineering, sales, customer service, manufacturing, finance, research, and other departments. It sounds like a fun, interdisciplinary job, but (at least in Silicon Valley) it's actually very tough. You're responsible for everything related to your product, but you have no direct control over the people who can make or break its success. The key skills are interpersonal: learning how to get along with different personality types in all those functions. Product managers listen closely to what those experts need and show empathy for whatever problems they are facing. Their goal is to fit into any internal subculture, winning the respect of the people in various functions.[5] A great product manager will have everyone supporting her, saying things like "She understands what we need and fights to get it for us."

The combination of learning, listening, and showing empathy to experts adds up to what I call the product manager mindset. Systems Leaders who start from a background in finance, sales, marketing, or other nontechnical functions often need to put in extra effort to become well versed in their company's technology. It's worth the time to do extra reading or research to be able to have well-informed, peer-to-peer discussions with the people who actually sling code and design machines. Former Nokia chairman Risto Siilasmaa wrote about why he took courses on AI and machine learning: "As a long-term CEO, I've gotten used to having things explained to me. Somebody else does the hard work and I can focus on figuring out the right questions. Sometimes CEOs and chairmen may feel that understanding the nuts and bolts of technology is in some way beneath their role, that it's enough for them to focus on 'creating shareholder value.' Alternatively, they may feel that they can't learn something seemingly complicated and therefore don't consider trying. Neither one is the entrepreneurial way."[6]

Stanford professor Amir Goldberg (my former coteacher for "Strategies of Effective Product Management") uses the term *network brokers* to describe this role of interacting with numerous different groups and building bridges between them. His research found that the most effective product managers subtly shifted the way they spoke and acted to fit into the distinct culture of each department, such as engineering, sales, or manufacturing. The more that they could adapt like chameleons in different group contexts, the more likely they were to rise in their careers and stay for long tenures.[7] Systems Leaders can benefit just as much by adapting their communications style to the unique listeners in front of them at any given moment.

When products were largely analog, the origin of competitive advantage was owning assets such as factories and land. A high volume of sales enabled the lowest cost basis of supply inputs. Product distribution was accomplished in a two-tier fashion, with distributors and retailers reaching a high number of customers, and product cycles that could be measured in years. But in a world where many more products have a digital component, great product managers know that production assets can be rented rather than purchased; that network effects can drive the economic value of a good or service; that companies can have intimate relationships with customers by selling directly and minimizing the use of channels; and that products can be easily updated via software. Even the way products are developed and delivered is changing, and must continue to change, in a world where each good and service has a digital aspect.

If a company is going to develop products differently due to having a digital component, Systems Leaders need to organize their companies with a different set of operating principles. They can use data to make decisions based on customer insights, relying less on intuition and hierarchy. They can push more decision-making authority down toward those who are closest to customers, so that changes can be implemented more quickly to serve customers better. And they can treat their IT departments not primarily as a cost center but as a revenue generator that creates opportunities for ongoing contact with customers, leading to desirable new products and services.

Products and Organizations Are Transformed in the Digital Era

PRODUCTS

Owning Assets	⟶ Renting Assets
Analog Products	⟶ Digital Products
Scale of Supply	⟶ Network Effects
Indirect Distribution	⟶ Direct Distribution
Regulatory Capture	⟶ Regulatory "Experimentation"
3+ Year Prod. Cycle	⟶ Daily Product Updates

ORGANIZATIONS

Efficiency (Six Sigma)	⟶ Responsiveness
Intuition Decisions	⟶ Information-based
Hierarchy	⟶ Decentralized
Designed for Risk	⟶ Designed for Upside
Management-Centric	⟶ Product-centric
IT as Cost Center	⟶ Revenue Generator

Systems Leaders may have more operational authority than product managers in some situations, in which case they can't complain about being accountable for everything while owning nothing. Nevertheless, it pays huge dividends to think like a product manager at all levels of an organization. Dive deeply into the technologies that underpin your products and your company's ecosystem. Listen closely to experts and show empathy for their concerns. When you must make a decision that upsets certain factions, your strong relationships ("She's one of us!") will soften the blow.

Embracing Risk During Uncertainty and Disruption

Financial theory says that in times of exceptional volatility, you should become extra cautious and adopt a "risk off" mindset. But

Systems Leaders generally have the opposite impulse. The more disruptive their situation, the more they go "risk on" and confront the source of the challenge, rather than passively waiting to see how things play out in their company or industry. They learn how to manage their own anxiety and that of their teams. The Systems Leaders we'll meet in the chapters ahead, whether disruptors or incumbent giants, all summon their courage for untested, risky strategies. They run *toward* disruptions the way firefighters train themselves to run into burning buildings.

One tactic for leading through uncertainty is to watch how you spend your time, because your people are watching. Your actions send a clear signal to the organization about what you consider important, regardless of what you might say in a speech or email blast. Andy Grove proved this in *Only the Paranoid Survive,* when he reprinted a week from the desk calendar of the CEO of a large multinational during a significant corporate inflection point, revealing how his leader allowed his time to be filled with lots of non-essential meetings and factory tours, while ignoring the crisis at hand.[8]

As mentioned previously, another tactic is to be mindful of the difference between skill and luck. Looking at your career so far, were all of your past successes really dependent on your talents and hard work, or were some due mainly to being in the right place at the right time? Acknowledging the role of luck won't diminish your accomplishments, but it will inoculate you against hubris when you go "risk on." (We'll return to this theme later in the book.)

Applying These Traits to the Five Major Cross-Pressures

All of these personal traits help Systems Leaders navigate the five major cross-pressures that I've introduced. We'll explore each of them at greater depth in the chapters ahead. The point to remember now is that, when it comes to cross-pressures, Systems Leaders consistently seek *both/and* solutions rather than looking at these as *either/or* dilemmas. For instance:

- With *priorities,* they strive to execute skillfully on today's operations, *while also* driving disruptive innovations that may not pay off for years to come.

- With *people,* they display strength and demand high standards, *while also* showing kindness, empathy, and humility.

- With *sphere of influence,* they find ways to support the internal needs of their own organization, *while also* navigating a complex external ecosystem of partners, customers, competitors, and regulators.

- With *geography,* they support their own country of origin in their approaches to markets, supply chains, and operations, *while also* embracing the opportunities offered by globalization.

- With *purpose,* they maintain fierce ambition for their own careers and the success of their organizations, *while also* acting with gravitas to model the greater good of acting as a statesman or stateswoman.

The common thread is that instead of lamenting the unfairness of such cross-pressures, they roll up their sleeves and confront them.

The more that Systems Leadership becomes a shared language within an organization, the more everyone begins to see not only their separate pieces of the puzzle but the entire puzzle. Frontline employees get better at grasping connections and opportunities that thinkers who stay in one narrow lane will miss. They also become more likely to adapt and grow, as internal and external pressures inevitably change the demands placed on them.

Coming Up

Now that we've concluded part 1, it's time to explore the five major cross-pressures in more detail and see how real Systems Leaders are navigating them. First up is the eternal conundrum of balancing today's priorities with tomorrow's.

Questions to Ponder

- Do you tend to see your company through one main functional perspective, or are you already pretty good at understanding and appreciating multiple perspectives?

- Do you have close relationships with others in different functions? Do they trust you, and do you trust them?

- Do you generally find operating at intersections to be easy or difficult?

- Have you ever worked as a product manager, or worked closely with one? If so, how might the product manager mindset be a useful way to approach your job?

PART 2

The Five Major Cross-Pressures and What to Do About Them

CHAPTER 4

Priorities:
Execution *and* Innovation

I believe that form follows function, but both follow emotion.

—Jochen Zeitz, chairman and CEO, Harley-Davidson

Prioritizing Today over Tomorrow

Juggling priorities is difficult in any sphere of life. Should you work late today to catch up on email, or log off at 4 PM to watch your kid's soccer game? Stick to your diet when out to dinner with friends, or try the mouthwatering special? Buy a practical, safe, fuel-efficient sedan, or splurge on the sports car of your dreams? Only you can say. As Harley-Davidson's Jochen Zeitz observed, all rational calculations are ultimately subordinate to emotion. That's especially true for fundamental questions about priorities: Why are we here? How should we define success? What sacrifices are worth making on the road to success?

Consider aerospace giant Boeing, which has spent years under a legal, regulatory, and public relations cloud due to a series of terrifying accidents and allegations of systemic negligence. While observers have studied Boeing's woes from the perspectives of engineering, quality control, regulatory compliance, and PR, I find it most useful to treat the company's travails as a failure of prioritization. When faced with the cross-pressure of investors angling for leadership to deliver higher profits and a tradition of "safety-first" innovation and operations, Boeing's C-suite recklessly decided to prioritize today over tomorrow.

In 2018 and 2019, two crashes of its 737 Max 8 model killed a combined 346 people. All Max 8 jets were grounded for almost two years, a huge financial blow. Boeing had to spend more than $2.5 billion in 2021 to settle charges of fraud, violating safety regulations, and inadequate disclosure of essential information. With the company's reputation in tatters, many airlines turned to Boeing's archrival, Airbus, to resupply their fleets.

Just as Boeing was beginning to recover from these setbacks, a door plug blew off a 737 Max 9 at 16,000 feet in January 2024, forcing an Alaska Airlines flight to make an emergency landing. A preliminary report by the National Transportation Safety Board said that four bolts meant to secure the door plug in place were missing before the panel blew off.[1] Then, just a few weeks later, a 747-8 cargo plane bound for Puerto Rico caught fire as the result of an engine failure, forcing an emergency landing in Miami. And in March 2024, a flight from San Francisco to Japan "lost a portion of landing gear tire during takeoff," damaging several parked cars.[2]

One might argue that such incidents were simply a run of bad luck. Nearly 100,000 flights take off and land worldwide each day, with virtually no serious problems. Rare exceptions could show up anywhere, and the airlines share responsibility for maintaining Boeing's products. But investigations by the Federal Aviation Administration (FAA) and Congress found that this wasn't bad luck; Boeing senior management had consistently dismissed or downplayed safety concerns raised by frontline employees, who saw that shortcuts and quick fixes were increasingly encouraged.

For instance, the company had told airlines and the FAA that pilots didn't require simulation training when upgrading from the previous model to the Max 8, which reduced Boeing's costs and improved sales. However, some experts believe such training would likely have prevented the 2018 and 2019 crashes. Subpoenaed internal communications revealed Boeing employees' widespread lack of faith in the 737 Max and complaints about top management prioritizing deadlines and cost-cutting over safety. One employee even emailed a colleague: "I don't know how to fix these things . . . it's systemic. Sometimes you have to let big things fail so that everyone can identify a problem."[3]

As Jeff Immelt bluntly observed, while working on a case study for our class: "Boeing had a bad culture, especially for a critical infrastructure business." For decades the company had prided itself on engineering excellence, operational perfectionism, and an obsession with safety. But a shift in priorities began with the 1997 acquisition of McDonnell Douglas, which brought an influx of new executives who focused on deadlines and profits, compared with Boeing veterans who had spent years absorbing the gospel of time-intensive, labor-intensive product development.

One of those McDonnell Douglas newcomers was Harry Stonecipher, who served as Boeing CEO from 2003 to 2005. Among other precedent-breaking moves, he began outsourcing the supply chain and manufacturing for the new 787 Dreamliner to save on development costs and shorten the timeline; this actually ended up costing Boeing more and taking longer while also reducing product quality. During Stonecipher's tenure the share price rose significantly, but at the cost of upending Boeing's traditional values. Yet he remained unapologetic, telling an interviewer in 2019,

"When people say I changed the culture of Boeing, that was the intent, so that it's run like a business rather than a great engineering firm."[4] This mindset endured through the next few CEO administrations, including those of Dennis Muilenburg (2015–19) and Dave Calhoun (2020–24), who both lost their jobs due to the scandals and failures to successfully address the company's problems.

Imagine an alternate history of the past two decades at Boeing, in which a team of Systems Leaders faced the same competitive and investor pressures to cut costs, increase sales, and speed up innovation. Rather than expecting employees to take shortcuts and suppress their concerns, this team might have stressed that product deadlines mattered less than Boeing's commitment to safety-first excellence. And they could have stressed that integrity equals strength, and that a century-old reputation can be ruined by a few years of reckless leadership (to paraphrase Warren Buffett).

Of course, hindsight is always 20/20. Keep that in mind as you read about various situations of conflicting priorities in this chapter, especially those in which today's execution is in tension with tomorrow's innovation. It's easy for outsiders to say, "Leadership should have done *this or that,* and then they would have avoided that failure." It's much harder to calculate trade-offs when a quarterly report is looming or your boss is demanding immediate results. But in the end such facts cannot be an excuse for failure.

Old and New Approaches to Balancing Execution and Innovation

I'm hardly the first to observe that even great leaders struggle with the cross-pressures of setting priorities—especially those of executing the current plan to its maximum potential while also devoting time and resources to innovation. Many scholars of business management have studied the tendency of companies to get stuck in processes and systems that make it extremely hard for new ideas and opportunities to take hold, while others have proposed models for how to go about it. For instance, Stanford's Charles A. O'Reilly III and Harvard's Michael Tushman introduced what they called "the ambidextrous organization" as a model for simultaneously exploiting opportunities in existing businesses while exploring new areas of potential growth.[5] Similarly, Stanford's Robert Burgelman offered a new model for concurrently optimizing core businesses while pursuing new ones.[6]

As valuable as such research has been, it was developed in an era when big companies kept their core and innovation teams separate. The leaders of existing business units were expected to deliver operational excellence—scaling as big as possible while maximizing efficiency and reliability. Meanwhile, innovation groups were often staffed by nonconformists who didn't think, talk, or even dress like the leaders of those core units.

In the worst cases, these two groups didn't respect each other at all. Operators would scorn innovators for chasing shiny new objects that often turned out to be mirages. In return, innovators would dismiss operators as out-of-touch dinosaurs, unable or unwilling to embrace whatever new tech seemed to be the next big thing. Even in the best-case scenario, these groups would collaborate only grudgingly, like hostile tribes facing a common enemy but without any mutual admiration. And transferring between such tribes would be difficult and rare.

To manage such tensions, interactions between operators and innovators were often managed by a single senior leader or a small group at the highest level of the corporation. Top management would attempt to keep peace between the tribes, minimize their battles over resources and priorities, and try to convince them that the real "enemy" was outside the organization.

These days, for all the reasons we explored in chapter 1, leaders at all levels are increasingly expected to excel at both execution *and* innovation. Those who develop only one or the other skill set are at a significant disadvantage in their quest for career advancement. On the other hand, Systems Leaders who develop a knack for both operating at scale and fostering innovation can thrive, and in fact can find their greatest satisfaction at that intersection.

Investing for Today *and* Tomorrow

One of the toughest kinds of decisions around priorities is investing across multiple time horizons (near-term and long-term) at the same time. When competing requests for human and financial resources all sound worthwhile, how are leaders supposed to make those choices?

During the typical budgeting process, leaders first try to match spending and resources across projects, functions, and long-term investments, and then they communicate those priorities to their employees, boards, and shareholders. These plans also drive the individual benchmarks and milestones for many employees, based on how well they are helping the company achieve its goals. For small companies, the deciding factor in allocation choices is usually simple: Don't run out of cash. If a startup still has not shipped its initial product, getting that product out the door is the obvious top priority; every other potential use of resources should be put on the back burner.

But as an organization grows and adds multiple product lines, setting priorities for resources becomes more complex. How should capital and personnel be invested across developing new products, improving existing products, making manufacturing more efficient, boosting customer support, experimenting with new marketing campaigns, and honing internal administration? Good cases can often be made for all those priorities. But capital is scarce, and adding head count is especially expensive given the challenges of attracting and retaining skilled talent. Calculating the risks associated with any long-term innovation can feel impossibly hard, given the combination of technical risk, execution risk, and market risk. Sometimes it can feel like pure guesswork.

Setting priorities becomes even more complex when leaders consider the needs and goals of their investors. The financial markets can have tough benchmarks and timelines for return on investment and be quick to punish companies that underperform expectations. Startups often face extreme pressure from their venture capitalists, who usually need to cash out their innovation funds in less than ten years so they can return capital to their limited partners.[*] For both startups and large companies, the liquidity of markets at any given moment can determine if investment capital is even available, and at what price. If all goes well, executives can choose their sources of capital (such as VC firms, private equity, the stock market, the bond market, or even angel investors), but larger companies may face activist shareholders who want to influence how the company's resources are deployed. And all sources of capital, public or private, aim to be on what is called the "efficient frontier" of risk and reward—they expect that higher-risk investments will come with the potential for higher rewards.

Systems Leaders need to be conversant in all of these financial subtleties, both within the company and when it comes to outside sources of capital. They can't afford simply to delegate budgeting and cash management to their finance department. They need to

---

[*] A limited partner is a person or entity that provides capital to venture capitalists (also referred to as general partners) for investment.

roll up their sleeves and dig into these issues from multiple per-spectives at once, including the talent capabilities of the labor force, the details of operational execution, the market requirements of customers, and the current state and future outlook of the financial markets. For today's leaders, understanding the nuances of your capital is now just as essential as understanding your products.

One leader who excels at managing the cross-pressure of com-peting time horizons is Pedro Earp, who spent eight years as the Chief Disruptive Growth Officer at Anheuser-Busch InBev, the global beer and beverage conglomerate. He spoke to my class in 2018 about trying to maximize the company's mass-market beer sales while simultaneously developing or acquiring new micro-brews to appeal to different markets and experimenting with bold new ways to deliver beer to customers.

Yet even for a Systems Leader like Earp, juggling innovation with operating at scale was tough. He told us that AB InBev was trying to do three things at once: develop innovations (such as ways of digitally measuring draft beer service in bars and online home delivery of beer), scale new innovations to become sustainable, and continue to drive the growth of already massive brands (such as Budweiser). Put simply: creating new things, growing small things, and making big things even bigger. The company was outstanding at the third competence but recognized an urgent need to improve at the first two. Part of Earp's mission was to "infect" the entire or-ganization with a stronger spirit of innovation—that was the spe-cific word chosen by then-CEO Carlos Brito. The ultimate goal was to make Earp's role as the head of an innovation team obsolete.

Earp did well enough that he was promoted to chief marketing officer in 2019, before leaving the company to pursue entrepre-neurship in 2022. His time at Anheuser-Busch InBev illustrates how even the biggest companies now face a cross-pressure over priorities that must be confronted head-on, not by a small group of individuals in the C-suite but by everyone with any decision-making authority. Inventing new things, growing small initiatives, and scaling existing businesses are all essential competencies, and the temptation for individuals to stick to just one of them should be resisted.

In the examples that follow, you'll see how the demands of the financial markets intertwine with the challenges of investing simultaneously for the near term and the long term, in terms of both money and attention.

Pursuing a New Kind of Customer *and* Catering to Loyalists

Jochen Zeitz, a German native and former longtime CEO of Puma, has been CEO of Harley-Davidson since 2020. He was brought in as a turnaround specialist to reinvent the iconic motorcycle manufacturer's expansion and innovation, following one of the worst stretches of underperformance in its 120-year history. A *New York Times* journalist assessed the company's declining fortunes in 2021: "Recent years have not been kind to Harley-Davidson. Its sales have sagged, its core customers have aged, and its push toward the electric future, while newly serious, has underwhelmed so far. In 2019, the last full year unaffected by the coronavirus, Harley shipped 218,000 motorcycles, earning $424 million in net income on $5.36 billion in revenue, healthy enough but well off its glory days."[7]

This decline wasn't exclusively a Harley problem. Sales across the entire U.S. motorcycle industry had been cut in half since 2006, the year they peaked at 1.1 million bikes. As the general manager of a Harley dealership in Marina del Rey, California, quipped:

"The Millennials are getting in too slow, and the baby boomers are leaving too fast. We need a new kind of customer."[8]

Zeitz was a bold choice to pursue that new kind of customer. Not only was he not American; he was exceptionally cosmopolitan and active in sustainability efforts and philanthropy in Africa, among other interests. But as a member of the board since 2007, he already knew the company well and was able to hit the ground running during his first year as CEO. He began with a full review of Harley's products, operations, and finances, and also of its very soul. Zeitz told me that when he took over, "We had a mission statement that was a full page long, and I thought, who has time to read that? So, I studied a lot about Harley-Davidson history, and it was clear that we aren't really about building machines. We stand for the timeless pursuit of adventure and freedom for the soul. That's our real mission, right?"[9]

Zeitz understood immediately that Harley faced a cross-pressure between competing priorities: honoring and extending its storied tradition on the one hand, while simultaneously pursuing the "new kind of customer" that the dealer in California was talking about. In a sense, this wasn't just a business challenge but a philosophical conundrum. Could electric motorcycles that reviewers described as quiet, unthreatening, and eco-friendly share a brand identity with the famously loud and aggressive Harley hogs?

Zeitz believed there was no real conflict from a brand point of view. "Our new vision followed that mission: leading through innovation, evolution, and emotion. We are an emotional brand—our product is highly emotional. I believe that form follows function, but both follow emotion, as [famous Harley designer] Willie G. Davidson said. So, we defined our goal as restoring Harley's place as the most desirable sport and lifestyle brand in the world." That vision led to an ambitious five-year plan called The Hardwire, which Zeitz unveiled in February 2021. It set bold targets for combining profitable growth with what Zeitz called "a reinvigorated culture of performance, efficiency, focus and speed."[10]

Electric motorcycles were a key component of Zeitz's turnaround plan, building on Harley's groundbreaking success with the LiveWire motorcycle. First released in 2019, the LiveWire was marketed to a younger, more urban, more affluent customer base. One reviewer called it "a bike that looks and feels as progressive as the company's new mode of thinking."[11]

But this innovation didn't sit well with some of Harley's most loyal and passionate fans, who wanted the company to focus on the features that had become synonymous with Harley bikes for decades. Such traditions include not just high-quality production but the raw excitement of bikes that roar loudly and assertively, enabling riders to feel kinship with icons like Marlon Brando, Evel Knievel, and the stars of *Easy Rider*.

Before Zeitz's arrival, tensions were rising between these two distinct customer segments. And in a country where mass-market brands like Starbucks, Bud Light, and Chick-Fil-A easily become culture war flashpoints, Harley might have been stepping into a minefield by pursuing innovations at odds with Harley loyalists. Zeitz, who describes himself as an "optimistic realist," was well aware of the importance of not alienating Harley's core customers. His study of the brand's history showed that Harley had never been coded as explicitly political, but rather as espousing freedom and other values associated with America more broadly. Both conservatives and liberals had always bought and loved Harleys, and Zeitz saw maintaining that inclusivity as a key part of his mission. Being forced to choose sides between Red and Blue America would be a potential disaster.

Thus, in 2022, Harley spun off LiveWire as a separate company, which made sense financially as well as culturally. As Zeitz saw it, "Electrification requires a huge investment. If we had applied the same investing principles to LiveWire that we applied to Harley, it would always be a fifth wheel on the wagon. And not only was there very little overlap between LiveWire customers and Harley customers, but also among investors. The kinds of investors who want to take a bigger risk on the future of EVs can now do that without being tied to our traditional operations. Now we have both a startup that can ride the transformation of the next ten, twenty, or thirty years, plus a stable organization that's been around for 120 years. And neither one has to compromise its principles or worry about alienating the other one's customers."

So far, this solution to a customer-driven cross-pressure is working for both Harley and LiveWire. Both have created the space to focus on both near-term and long-term objectives. For now at least, Zeitz seems to have found a way to balance those priorities, while delivering on both execution and innovation.

Maintaining Current Competencies *and* Mastering New Ones

Accenture was born in the 1950s as a small consulting division of the prominent accounting firm Arthur Andersen. In 1989, Arthur Andersen and Andersen Consulting split into sister companies with shared ownership. The two formally broke ties in 2000, and Andersen Consulting rebranded as Accenture in 2001—just in time to avoid being tarnished by the Enron scandal, which destroyed Arthur Andersen.[12] A quarter century later, Accenture has grown into a giant player in technology-driven consulting, with 743,000 employees serving more than 9,000 clients in 120 countries. Its global operations span more than 200 cities and generated more than $64 billion in revenue in 2023.[13] That makes it one of the top ten global consulting firms, with a focus on IT strategy, cloud services, artificial intelligence, global systems integration, information security, supply chains, and digital advertising.

Julie Sweet joined the firm as general counsel in 2010; her legal background gave her a rare and valuable perspective among colleagues who were mostly MBAs or technologists. She became CEO of its North American division in 2015 and global CEO in 2019. Along the way she has helped lead a dramatic expansion and transformation of Accenture's services, from primarily a back-end integrator of existing technologies to a pioneer of cutting-edge B2B services. She has repeatedly ranked high on *Fortune*'s annual list of the 100 most powerful women in business, including being named number one in 2020.[14]

Sweet combines the essential skills of a Systems Leader: predicting and preparing for the future, adopting a product manager mindset, managing the context of her changing ecosystem, and staying calm in the face of tough competition. She prides herself on maintaining a laser focus on the core mission of serving clients as their needs change. Everything other than customer focus has been fair game for reinvention, including Accenture's org chart, success metrics, and compensation practices. Sweet has been willing to part ways with senior leaders who were unable or unwilling to adapt during the firm's reinvention.

As she told my class in 2019: "Everything about the services we provide to our clients has changed. Eight years ago, we were less than 10 percent doing digital, cloud, and security. Today it's over 60 percent. And in order to drive that, we've fundamentally transformed all of Accenture. The most fundamental change is the mindset. Eight years ago, we were very proud of being fast followers and light on investment. Today, we're an innovation-led company and we deeply invest in skills and capabilities."[15]

At that time Sweet was especially proud of how Accenture had become an unlikely leader in digital advertising, having developed expertise in data-driven analytics and consumer targeting. They had set up a separate division to offer those services and compete with major advertising agencies. As the head of this Accenture Interactive unit told *The Wall Street Journal,* they might not be the place to go for a clever, *Mad Men*–style car commercial, but they had the expertise to help an automaker reinvent its car-buying experience and target the exact customers it sought.[16]

But just a few years later, it has become clear that Accenture can't be innovation-driven on *every* new technology, business process, or strategic method that clients might be demanding. As of this writing, generative AI is at the top of that list. Many of the firm's clients worry about being left behind on AI and are clamoring for guidance from trusted advisers. If Accenture can't deliver high-quality assistance in a timely fashion, many clients will turn to some other consulting firm—even if that means abandoning a long-standing relationship with Accenture.

So, Sweet's biggest current cross-pressure on priorities is maintaining and extending Accenture's existing competencies while also adding new expertise to serve clients who feel their own pressures at an unprecedented level. She recognizes that these challenges are tougher—and the stakes are higher—than they were just a half decade ago. As she recently told me: "While technology has obviously gone through a lot of evolutions over the last forty years, the current AI revolution is of an entirely different magnitude. That's on top of dealing with continued slow growth, post-pandemic government policies, and new economic issues that haven't existed in decades, such as sustained inflation. Then there's geopolitics as both an opportunity and a challenge. For instance, manufacturing in the United States is having a renaissance in no small part due to geopolitical tensions. So, I do think that the totality of what CEOs are managing today is significantly different by several degrees than when I became CEO in 2019."[17]

Sweet is not merely juggling execution and innovation internally; she's also helping Accenture's clients get better at doing the same juggle. For instance, the firm recently acquired Udacity, one of the first providers of massive open online courses (MOOCs). That's a sign of how dramatically education is changing, as well as how MOOC technology might become a core way to help companies and countries upgrade the knowledge and skills of their employees and citizens, especially on rapidly changing subjects such as AI. If this new teaching infrastructure can help Accenture's consultants stay on the cutting edge, they in turn can help their clients' employees keep up as well. It's a nontraditional yet intriguing move for an elite B2B consulting firm, much like digital advertising was a decade ago.

Preparing for the Future Without Giving Up on the Present

ConocoPhillips CEO Ryan Lance's primary cross-pressure is thorny, even existential, in scope: How do you lead a major energy company for success built around fossil fuels today, while also planning and investing for a future driven by clean energy? He knows that for the foreseeable future, the vast majority of his company's revenue will continue to come from oil and natural gas, while only a small portion will come from alternative energy sources such as solar and wind power. This is unavoidable since we are facing a shortage of energy globally, due to the increasing demands of developing countries and new technologies such as AI. Now in his early sixties, Lance will be selling mostly oil and gas until his retirement, and his successor almost certainly will as well. The company probably won't derive a majority of its revenue from green energy until his successor's successor is CEO.

The big question for Lance is how much to invest in green energy infrastructure now, versus maximizing short-term profits instead. As a Systems Leader with a strong sense of stewardship, Lance isn't kicking the can down the road. He's strategizing and executing on multiple time horizons at the same time, doing his best to ensure that ConocoPhillips will be well positioned for the future while still meeting its current operational and financial commitments.

Lance isn't worried about his reputation with Wall Street or his future career prospects; he's worried about the future of his company. At the same time, he's not going to overinvest in green energy in a rush of panic. He's looking for the sweet spot between doing too much and too little—between moving too quickly and too slowly toward the energy transition. This balancing act requires a combination of farsightedness and resoluteness in the face of potential criticism on all sides, from climate change activists to financial analysts.

I saw Lance's combination of those essential qualities when he spoke to my class in April 2020, during the extreme COVID-driven shock to the global economy. On the day of his guest appearance, the price of crude oil actually went negative for the first time. I jokingly asked him if this meant that I could drive to my local gas station, fill up my tank, and ask them to give me money. But the plunging price of oil was no joke—it was an unprecedented, mind-bending crisis for ConocoPhillips. Lance was resolute that day, determined to lead his company safely through this shock and into whatever new normal emerged on the other side.

He reminded my students that while the energy industry was often maligned as being stuck in its ways, it was in fact a hotbed of constant innovation, even in traditional fossil fuels. For instance,

ConocoPhillips had the ability to drill a hole two miles down, go horizontal another two miles, and then come up two miles and exit the ground within one foot of its targeted position. Such innovation is essential because oil and natural gas will remain part of the global energy solution for another half century. Alternative sources of energy are promising in the future, but for at least the next few decades, humanity also needs to make traditional energy sources cleaner and more efficient, so we can meet the growing global demand for power without doing additional damage to the environment.

Lance also stressed that controlling costs is absolutely critical for his company because the prices ConocoPhillips can charge for its commodity products are determined by global markets. With virtually no pricing power at its disposal, the company has to focus on innovation to keep up with (and hopefully surpass) its competition on efficiency. It must also stay nimble in the face of unexpected changes to government regulations around the world, as well as possible shocks from another global pandemic or some other external crisis.

All these innovation opportunities make it ironic that many of today's young technologists and business leaders don't even consider joining the traditional energy industry. Yet there may be no better career opportunity if you truly care about shaping the world of the future. Lance sees part of his mission as improving his industry's image, and he certainly succeeded with my students. One of them even emailed me the next day: "I never thought I would like the CEO of an oil company."

Satisfying Religious *and* Secular Customers

Adel Al-Majed took over as CEO of Boubyan Bank, an Islamic bank in Kuwait, in 2009. This was a somewhat risky career move because he left a very senior position (deputy CEO of consumer banking) at the National Bank of Kuwait, which at the time was one of the largest banks in the Middle East, with more than $44 billion in assets. In contrast, Boubyan Bank was the smallest bank in Kuwait and was struggling to get through the global financial crisis.[18]

Al-Majed and his new leadership team recognized that Boubyan faced a cross-pressure around the unique challenges of doing banking in accordance with Islamic Sharia law. Islamic banking prohibits usury, known as *riba,* and some religious scholars have concluded that charging or receiving any kind of interest is a sin. In order to serve their religiously observant customers, Islamic banks figured out ways to avoid directly paying or receiving interest.

For example, someone seeking a Sharia-compliant loan would identify the car they wanted to buy to an Islamic bank. After going through a standard credit review, the bank would set up a *murabaha* (cost-plus) contract with the customer. The bank would then buy the car from the dealer, and the customer would rebuy it from the bank at a higher price, with payment in installments over a set number of months. The result was almost exactly like a conventional loan; the monthly bills added up to more than the dealer's price, and the customer would not officially own the car until the contract was paid off. But those payments had the legal and religious status of 100 percent principal, with no interest.

Islamic banks used similar arrangements to offer Sharia-compliant versions of deposit accounts and investments. The market for such arrangements was huge; more than $2.5 trillion in assets were managed by Sharia-compliant financial institutions in 2018, across more than sixty countries. Boubyan thus had a strong incentive to maintain the loyalty of religiously conservative customers.

On the other hand, if Boubyan was going to grow and widen its customer base, it had to offer more than Sharia compliance as a selling point. Younger customers, in particular, wanted the same things that banking customers around the world wanted: more digital and mobile banking options, faster and more satisfying customer service, and a bigger retail presence. As Al-Majed recalled in August 2020, "If we could offer excellent service and give customers everything they got from conventional banks (products, services, experience) and add an Islamic flavor to it, maybe we can become the bank of choice."[19]

Research showed that potential Kuwaiti customers could be segmented into three groups. An estimated 10 to 15 percent were extremely liberal and avoided Islamic banks out of principle. Another 10 to 15 percent were extremely religious and would *only* bank with Islamic banks. But for the vast majority of the country, Sharia adherence was a bonus, not a requirement. They would be happy to choose an Islamic bank, but only if it was also competitive on product offerings, customer service, and innovation.

A commitment to competing both on religious compliance and secular benefits has guided the bank's strategy since Al-Majed's arrival. Retail banking represented just 1 percent of Boubyan's assets in 2008, when it had just ten branches. Al-Majed made an early decision to greatly expand that branch footprint. As he noted in 2020, "I agreed that the future is digital. But I wasn't going to wait around for customers to change. It was a controversial decision, but I had conviction. While most banks were closing branches, we were opening new ones. I told our CFO we might be closing some of them in 10 years, but right now we're growing and can't afford to wait."[20]

At the same time, the bank invested heavily in innovations that appealed to tech-savvy Kuwaiti Millennials. For instance, Boubyan became one of the first banks in the world to offer cardless ATM withdrawals, allowing customers to use their smartphone app to generate a secure code that would authorize an ATM to dispense cash. Such digital investments turned out to be just as impactful as those that went toward building more physical branches.

Similarly, Boubyan's corporate banking division began to compete with secular business banks on their own terms, with Sharia compliance positioned as a bonus rather than the main selling point. As Abdulsalam Al-Saleh, deputy CEO for corporate banking, put it, "I don't want people to come to Boubyan just because it's Islamic. I want them to come because it's a good bank with efficient processes and great customer service."[21] Initiatives to help corporate customers included streamlining bureaucratic processes, speeding up loan closings by making them fully digital, and diversifying the bank's loan portfolio to serve a wider, and cumulatively less risky, range of Kuwaiti businesses.

As a result of pursuing modernization along all these vectors without sacrificing Sharia compliance, Boubyan has thrived. By 2020, its assets reached $20 billion, up from just $4.6 billion in 2010, making it the nation's third-largest bank. It had captured nearly 50 percent of young Kuwaitis as customers, compared to near zero a decade earlier. And it was consistently ranking first in customer satisfaction across all Kuwaiti banks. These successes paved the way for future growth beyond Kuwait, and potentially across the rest of the Islamic world.

Placing Huge Bets *and* Surviving Quarter-to-Quarter

In chapter 1 we saw that 23andMe struggled with an intense cross-pressure around priorities, driven in part by having two distinct kinds of investors with different goals. Risk-averse stockholders would have preferred to see the company maximize its consumer

DNA testing business and related services, which generated modest but stable revenues. More ambitious investors saw the consumer business as a drag on the company's high-risk/high-reward pharmaceutical research and development, taking advantage of its unmatched proprietary database of genomic and health data.

CEO Anne Wojcicki tried to keep both groups satisfied while her company worked to commercialize the data it has collected from more than 14 million DNA tests. She resisted pressure to split the consumer and drug development units into separate companies, because a split would likely hurt their aggregate results. But in the meantime, 23andMe's market cap declined by as much as 98 percent since it went public in 2021—"From $6 billion to nearly $0," as *The Wall Street Journal* headlined a tough analysis in February 2024. That article noted that three rounds of layoffs had cut a quarter of the staff, including half of the drug development team, and that the company had never reported a profit.[22]

It's been quite a roller coaster since Wojcicki and her cofounder launched 23andMe in 2006. Her vision was huge from the start: "Using genetic data to revolutionize healthcare."[23] And in some ways that vision has already come to pass; few would have predicted that 14 million people would give any company permission to do research with their ancestry, health history, genotype, and phenotypic data. But Wojcicki also believed passionately that building such a massive database would enable scientists to unlock powerful new drugs, potentially targeting diseases ranging from cancer to asthma.

Back when the startup was still private, her vision and passion impressed many skeptics. For instance, Wojcicki told me about her 2017 pitch to Sequoia Capital, after it had declined to join 23andMe's first funding round and instead backed a competitor. She had declared: "I'm here to tell you about what we're doing, but I'm not here to try to win you over. We are going to win. We have been through a lot and everyone dismissed us. If you are looking for an IPO or a short-term exit, you are not the right match for us. I'm looking for people who genuinely buy into the vision and want to be along for the ride, but it's going to be super bumpy. I can't promise you timelines. I can't promise you exactly how things are going to happen. But I promise you the vision is stable."[24]

Unfortunately for investors, "super bumpy" turned out to be an understatement. For instance, Sequoia ultimately invested $145 million in 23andMe and held all of its equity for a long time, which was worth just $18 million in early 2024.[25] That decline came despite a widely praised 2018 drug development joint venture with GlaxoSmithKline (GSK), which brought in an additional $300 million in funding plus operational and research muscle to optimize R&D. Scientists at both partnering companies were optimistic that 23andMe's proprietary genomic dataset would enable discovery of safer, more effective "precision" medicines that could target narrower patient subgroups for numerous diseases.

But even with a priceless dataset, plenty of capital, and world-class scientists, drug development is still extremely hit-or-miss. Typical approval rates are just 9 to 14 percent for drug candidates that have already reached the tough milestone of phase I clinical trials. While pharma companies can earn tens of *billions* from a single blockbuster drug (think Lipitor, Zoloft, or Viagra), every failure along the way can lose tens of millions.

Given that ongoing need for capital, going public via a SPAC (special purpose acquisition company) seemed like a good idea in 2021, when SPACs offered startups higher valuations than later-stage private investors as well as an easier path to becoming public than the traditional Wall Street IPO process. But numerous startups that chose the SPAC route found their stocks overvalued and subject to steep declines. Many were also underprepared for the scrutiny of what Wojcicki called the "daily report card" of the stock ticker. In retrospect, 23andMe probably should have resisted the SPAC fad and waited to go public until it had at least one successful drug as proof of concept. As *The Wall Street Journal* noted, "23andMe says it has found more than 50 'drug candidates.' So far two have made it to early-stage human trials. Later this year, data could be released that will show whether one of them works."[26]

By September 2024, the stock hovered around an all-time low and Wojcicki tried to take the company private again, despite the objections of her own board over how she handled the process. By the time you read this, the company may have been acquired, gone bankrupt, or otherwise lost its independence. Or it may be on the road to a comeback that will reward those who kept faith in its mission.

But a more interesting question is whether our estimation of Wojcicki's leadership should also depend on the success or failure of those drugs. I have known her for years and have often called her a good example of a Systems Leader. I don't see any reason to withdraw my opinion just because the company's scientists did not produce the next Lipitor or Humira. When you take a big swing at disrupting a huge industry, you can do everything possible to navigate conflicting priorities yet still fall short. Leaders always need to make decisions with imperfect information, which means that getting it wrong sometimes is inevitable. It's easy but often unfair to criticize any decision in hindsight.

Systems Leadership is not a panacea, nor an inoculation against making unwise decisions with partial data. Furthermore, as we've seen, the context for big decisions can seemingly shift overnight. Tech trends and entire industries can become extremely hot, but then suddenly go ice cold. Startup capital can be cheap and abundant during a prolonged period of easy money, until a spike in interest rates sends investors running for safety. Innovative financing models such as SPACs can be widely embraced, then just as quickly rejected when their drawbacks become apparent.

Part of Systems Leadership is knowing that some of your biggest bets may fail, yet still finding the emotional strength to get back up and keep going. As Wojcicki told me back in 2019, "We'll make lots of wrong decisions. . . . You only figure that out by trial and error. But I believe in the long run that the right thing to do will pay off."[27]

Medical schools teach future doctors how to cope with the deaths of their patients; great business schools and mentors rarely teach future leaders how to cope with the loss of their investors' capital, their employees' jobs, and their own reputations. Not every business story can be a "hero's journey" that ends in triumph, and not every setback is temporary. But that doesn't mean the journey wasn't worth the effort.

Questions to Ponder

- How does your organization treat employees who raise concerns about safety or other important issues? Did the Boeing example of a "don't rock the boat" culture sound familiar?

- Have you ever felt that your company's budgeting process underfunded innovation or other long-term priorities? Did anyone try to change those priorities?

- Do you think Harley-Davidson did the right thing by spinning off its LiveWire division, rather than trying to transform the main Harley brand around sustainability?

- Julie Sweet draws a significant distinction between being an innovator and a fast follower. How significant do you consider the difference? When is it okay to be a fast follower and when might it put a company at a disadvantage?

▪ We often talk about the importance of targeting specific kinds of customers. Do you think Boubyan Bank took too big a risk by trying to target both religious conservatives and other consumers who were less religiously observant?

▪ Do you think it's fair or unfair to judge a leader like Anne Wojcicki strictly on the financial performance of her company or business unit? Is it possible to be a great leader at a failed company, and vice versa?

CHAPTER 5

People:
Strength *and* Empathy

Welcome to Crotonville

Long before I joined General Electric in 2004, I had heard about its famous leadership training center in Crotonville, New York. Founded in 1956, it was the country's first "corporate university," offering managers some of the best executive education available from a private company. Even GE's website acknowledges the "hubris" of investing significant resources to build a dedicated facility aiming to create "the best managed company in the world."[1]

Despite Crotonville's long reputation for excellence, I still wasn't prepared for my first invitation to attend one of its three-week training programs for new executives. From the moment I arrived, I was impressed that the place was bigger, better run, and more serious than I'd expected. In my cohort of rising mid-career leaders we were expected to apply ourselves toward significant learning and skills improvement. The company hired top-tier faculty from around the world to teach us concepts from product management to team dynamics to launching new initiatives. It brought in prominent guest speakers, including CEOs of other Fortune 500 companies and members of GE's own top leadership. The main lecture hall was designed as a circular pit (universally known as The Pit), very much like those where Stanford and Harvard MBA students were trained.

Beyond the coursework, the staff at Crotonville treated us very well. The dorm-style residence halls weren't luxurious, but they were comfortable and well maintained. The meals were much better than college dorm food (it was easy to put on a lot of weight at Crotonville), and we were encouraged to rotate our dining partners and network with colleagues we didn't know. Then each night we were encouraged to linger in the lounge and continue our conversations over a drink from the open bar.

I tried to estimate how much the company spent on these courses, including all the staff costs, room and board, the faculty and guest speakers, plus the cost of flying many of us in from around the world. Then I multiplied this by several dozen such Crotonville programs throughout the year, for leaders at different levels. It had to add up to hundreds of millions of dollars. Was it worth it? Well, I went home with a lot of new knowledge, many new professional relationships, a clearer head after three weeks away from the daily grind—and a deep appreciation for my employer. In the grand scheme of GE's nearly $180 billion in annual revenue, my $350 million division was small potatoes. Yet the company had made me feel special, respected, and well cared for, and in return I felt my loyalty rising.

In retrospect, my warm and fuzzy feelings should have been tempered by the downside of forcing my wife to become a solo parent with three little kids while I was away. At one point during that first trip, when our kids were particularly acting up, she said on the phone with extreme exasperation, "What kind of company makes people leave their families for three weeks and doesn't make it easy to return on the weekends?" By today's standards, Crotonville was far from family friendly. It was still geared towards the two-parent, single-income families that were stereotypical in an earlier era, rather than dual-career families and single parents of the twenty-first century.

Another notable juxtaposition strikes me in hindsight. While spending hundreds of millions of dollars to train and support mid-level and senior leaders, GE was simultaneously known for an unforgiving culture of high expectations and strict accountability. Executives and frontline workers who repeatedly missed their numbers were let go with little hesitation. And the company was infamous for its "ranking and rating" performance evaluations, in which the lowest 10 percent of the workforce was supposed to be "coached out" every year. Crotonville was officially named the John F. Welch Leadership Development Center, honoring the legendary ex-CEO whom the press had nicknamed "Neutron Jack" in the 1980s because of his penchant for mass layoffs.

How could "the best managed company in the world" be simultaneously so tough and so benevolent? As we just saw with the tension between today's and tomorrow's priorities, the tension between leading with empathy or strength has to be resolved with a mindset of *both/and,* not *either/or.* In this chapter we'll explore how Systems Leaders are navigating that tension in their approaches to the training, development, and other needs of their people.

The Two Kinds of People in the World

One provocative assertion I often make when teaching is that there are two kinds of people in the world: those who have hearts and those who don't. Students and executives usually chuckle awkwardly at this statement, wondering where I am going. I then share that many leaders look at changing technology and changing markets and realize that a lot of jobs in their companies will inevitably be eliminated within the next few years, and it's not hard to predict which jobs will go away. The question is how the executives react to this realization.

Leaders who "have hearts" experience empathy for those currently in jobs that will be disappearing, seeing individual faces and hearing individual names in their minds. Such leaders think of the men and women in their organizations as flesh-and-blood humans. They worry about employees losing jobs that feed their children, keep roofs over their heads, and provide health insurance, not to mention (hopefully) supplying a sense of satisfaction and meaning.

Other leaders see the job elimination through a cooler lens, less concerned for those affected. They embrace "creative destruction" as a fundamental aspect of how capitalistic systems work. Austrian economist Joseph Schumpeter wrote about the inevitability that new technologies and advancements will destroy what came before.[2] For instance, there used to be great demand for skilled telegraph operators and folks who could add columns of numbers quickly with just a pencil—until more cost-effective technologies devalued those skills. Leaders with this perspective focus not on the hardships of the unemployed but on the numerous new jobs created by the same forces of change. They believe employees simply must adapt or be left behind, and there's no point in getting upset about it—everyone owns their individual career. They see the latest disruptions as just the continuation of the human experience, going all the way back to our hunter-gatherer ancestors. Still others may only care about job cuts for the sake of cost reduction, never mind the "creative" part of the destruction.

For the purposes of Systems Leadership, it doesn't matter which type of person you are in my (admittedly reductive) shorthand. You need to invest in your people whether you have a heart or not, for at least three major reasons.

First, it's often both easier and cheaper to retrain a current employee than to recruit and hire a new one with the skills you now need. According to research by the Society for Human Resource Management, "Employers will need to spend the equivalent of six to nine months of an employee's salary in order to find and train their replacement. That means an employee salaried at $60,000 will cost the company [an extra] $30,000 to $45,000. . . . Other research shows the average costs could be even higher. In a study conducted by the Center for American Progress, the cost of losing an employee can be anywhere from 16 percent of their salary for hourly employees, to 213 percent of the salary for a highly trained position."[3] Thus, reskilling a current employee will usually be less expensive than recruiting a new one, even if such reskilling costs $10,000 or more. Even if you *only* care about the bottom line, it is in your economic interest to invest in the development of your people.

Second, investing in retraining and other forms of continuing education can have an intangible but enormous impact on workplace morale, enthusiasm, and discretionary effort. Imagine the emotional impact of learning that your company is addressing an urgent need for more AI experts by choosing a group of promising current employees to go for supplemental training. Now imagine hearing instead that the company has posted numerous open positions for external AI specialists, which will be hard to fill without extremely high-paying salary offers. Worse, to pay for those new hires a major wave of layoffs will begin shortly.

Third, institutional knowledge is often undervalued, because (like morale) it can be hard to measure. While most leaders prioritize new ideas, new talent, and new opportunities, Systems Leaders also appreciate the perspectives of those who have confronted a wide range of past challenges.

Whether they "have hearts" or not, leaders must see employees as a resource to be invested in to advance the needs of the company. Systems Leaders take advantage of cost-saving opportunities without treating their people like replaceable cogs in a machine. At the same time, however, they believe fully in holding people accountable to high standards. They would say it's a false choice to frame strong management and compassionate management—hard heads and soft hearts—as opposites. Great leaders aspire to both.

With this framing, the paradox of Crotonville isn't really a paradox at all. GE was just an especially prominent example of simultaneously showing great care for its people while also holding them to extremely high expectations of consistent excellence.

"Learning Is the New Pension"

Author and business strategist Heather E. McGowan came up with a catchy slogan to capture this imperative: "Learning is the new pension." She noted that while automation has been widely seen as a threat to jobs for several decades, far fewer anticipated the threat posed by "atomization," which she defines as "separating a task from a job and having it done by a human in isolation, outside the envelope of employment, often using platforms like Uber, Fiverr, Upwork, and TaskRabbit."[4] This meant that far more jobs were endangered than people had anticipated, if even fully human tasks could be atomized away from the security and benefits of full-time employment. This type of work has been commonly referred to as the "gig economy."

Atomization elevated the urgency of helping just about everyone continuously deepen their knowledge and skills ("upskilling") and apply their existing knowledge, skills, and experience into new domains ("reskilling"). McGowan estimated that the average worker should be investing as much as an hour a day on reskilling and upskilling to stay ahead of the forces that might eliminate their jobs. Though that might seem excessive, she noted, "In the past we learned one time in order to work; now, we must work in order to learn continuously.... The reality is that your job is moving, and if you are not, it may be moving away from you."[5]

The big question, of course, is who should pay for all that upskilling and reskilling. As with retirement savings, the three viable contenders are individuals, governments, or employers. Most individuals find it hard to find the time, resources, and personal discipline to self-direct their own upskilling and reskilling. Governments can offer only partial solutions, with their limited budgets and the fact that formal education stops for most people after high school or university.

This leaves the onus on companies to close the skills gap. Just as employers during the post–World War II era began to lure workers with generous pensions, and later with generous matching of 401(k) plans, today's companies can attract and retain talent by offering ongoing education for more diverse career arcs. From almost any leader's perspective, treating learning as the new pension is a smart investment. All else being equal, talented people will prefer an employer that acts like it cares about their future over one that clearly doesn't. For most workers under forty, retirement is an abstraction in the distant future, but upskilling and reskilling are an urgent imperative for all employees. You can't expect the skills you acquired in high school or college to carry you all the way through to retirement.

Design Organizations for the Future of Work

Training like that provided at corporate learning centers like Crotonville, or envisioned by Heather McGowan, is only one aspect of confronting the cross-pressure around people. Anticipating the future of work in designing (or redesigning) an organization encompasses a range of essential decisions, including:

- To what degree should we be a virtual or an in-person company?

- What should we produce ourselves versus buying from outside vendors?

- What services and functions should remain internal and which should be outsourced?

- Where will new jobs be created internally and which jobs will be destroyed?

- Where will investment in human capital lead to more profits, versus where should we let go of certain tasks and people?

Coming out of the COVID pandemic, every knowledge-based company was forced to wrestle with the implications of that dramatic disruption. Those that had successfully gone remote in 2020 by using new collaboration tools had to consider which aspects of the so-called "new normal" could or should become permanent. By 2023, debates were raging about how much in-person collaboration was optimal for results, with leaders landing at different points on the wide spectrum between "Everyone needs to be back in the office every day!" and "Let's stay virtual forever and ditch our office expenses!" Employees have shown a similarly wide range of opinions; some want to permanently stop commuting and time spent in the office; others wish the workplace could return as much as possible to 2019.

Meanwhile, the aftermath of COVID also drove a spate of coverage about disengaged employees, especially those younger than roughly thirty-five. Whereas in the past, junior people mostly accepted that hard work and overtime were the ticket to advancing their careers, researchers now noted a distinct change in mindset toward lack of ambition and "quiet quitting."[6] Many also increasingly embraced the concept of the portfolio career or portfolio lifestyle, in which employees devote time and attention to a "side hustle" that augments their income and perhaps also keeps them intellectually or creatively stimulated. Some Systems Leaders found that they could satisfy these impulses by letting people try multiple roles simultaneously within their company. If people want more than one kind of role rather than pouring everything into their main job, why not let them scratch that itch internally without being forced to seek part-time work or launch solo businesses?

As we'll see in the examples that follow, Systems Leaders at all levels need to have a point of view on the major questions surrounding the future of work. What will be required to deliver great goods and services to your customers? What will your labor force want and demand? And how can your organization be redesigned to take advantage of these trends rather than being damaged or destroyed by them?

There Are Many Ways to Invest in People

Numerous leaders at all levels already embrace the urgency of developing people. Many are finding creative ways to pursue similar goals while maintaining high standards for excellence.

For instance, Julie Sweet at Accenture, whom we met in the previous chapter, encourages upskilling by having her workforce lean into automation instead of fearing it. By gamifying the process of automating existing jobs, she told me Accenture had retrained more than 200,000 workers in digital, cloud, and security, and would continue to push continuous learning while retaining institutional knowledge. "We've spent over $1 billion on education so far."[7]

Amazon drew attention in 2019 when it announced a $700 million initiative to retrain as many as 100,000 U.S. employees for new jobs that would be more in demand by 2025. As many as a third of the company's warehouse workers and delivery drivers would get the chance to move into higher skilled roles such as "data mapping specialist, data scientist, solutions architect and business analyst, as well as logistics coordinator, process improvement manager and transportation specialist."[8] This was one of the largest corporate retraining initiatives ever launched, including a new Amazon Technical Academy (for employees without tech skills), a new Associate2Tech program for fulfillment center workers, and other initiatives.[9]

While Amazon framed that $700 million pledge in terms of generosity, perhaps to counter bad PR about tough treatment of warehouse and delivery workers, the company also had a strong incentive to gain an edge in creating a pipeline of highly skilled workers. In September 2021, Amazon increased its pledge to $1.2 billion to give 300,000 employees access to education and skills-training programs, including college tuition for frontline employees, as part of this Upskilling 2025 initiative. And it continued to expand its range of programs, among them an Amazon Technical Apprenticeship that offered "paid and intensive classroom training along with apprenticeships."[10] This magnitude and range of investment strikes me as much more than a PR stunt.

But you don't need to be Amazon to sponsor significant employee development. Petronas, which is Malaysia's sovereign energy company and one of its largest employers, built an amazing leadership center for executive education. When they invited me to Kuala Lumpur for a teaching session, I was impressed by the high-quality facilities, which felt like a more modern version of Crotonville—an inspiring place to both learn and teach. I was even more impressed by the smart, thoughtful, engaged Petronas executives who were hungry for knowledge. The company faces steep challenges in attracting capital now that investors are gravitating toward clean energy instead of oil and gas, which are still essential in developing nations like Malaysia. Petronas urgently needs innovative thinking and is willing to invest heavily to develop such thinking among its existing leaders.

Another big company with an impressive commitment to its people is the OCP Group, Morocco's state-owned phosphate rock miner, phosphoric acid manufacturer, and fertilizer producer. It's the country's largest employer, responsible for a natural resource essential to Morocco's economy. OCP created and finances the Mohammed VI Polytechnic University (UM6P), which launched in 2013 and has an estimated endowment of $213 million.[11] The university isn't exclusively for OCP employees, but there's a close relationship between the two, for their mutual benefit as well as the nation's greater good.

Similarly, I've been impressed by TELUS, the Canadian telecommunications and information technology conglomerate. From CEO Darren Entwistle on down, the leadership is strongly committed to developing its people, including via investments in various education programs. Not only do they consistently engage with various global business schools for training their top 250 leaders, but TELUS also deploys a Directors Leadership Forum to enable the next one thousand or so leaders to receive an abbreviated version of the same training in their home cities. I joined two of my Stanford colleagues on a 2024 road trip that included sessions in Montreal, Toronto, Calgary, and Vancouver. The goal was not just to teach new skills and competencies but also to encourage new mindsets that could reshape the company's overall culture.

These examples, in widely different countries and industries, don't all approach continuing education or training in similar ways. But the key commonality is that they all recognize the power of investing in talent for the long run. Organizations that see training as a luxury tend to slash its budget during tough times, but such cuts may be sacrificing tomorrow's benefits for today's frugality. You can't count on the public school system or even universities to keep your current or future employees up to speed with constant change.

Flex: "I Don't See It as a Zero-Sum Game"

In chapter 1 we saw how Revathi Advaithi, the Austin-based CEO of Flex, faces the cross-pressure of maximizing the output of her global workforce of 140,000-plus while showing empathy and concern for their needs. Because Flex is a tech-driven manufacturing and supply chain company, this cross-pressure plays out most prominently around the overlap of innovation and job obsolescence. Advaithi is clear-eyed in accepting that Flex can only compete by fully and constantly embracing new hardware and software solutions. As she put it, "We can't have blinders on and say that this doesn't exist and this is not coming towards us."[12]

But because she cares deeply about her people, she also puts a lot of energy into taking care of those employees whose jobs will be impacted by new, advanced manufacturing technologies. It's easy to talk about retraining and reskilling in the abstract, but much harder when most of your 140,000 employees work in factories.

"Our factories are constantly changing because of the number and variety of customer programs we support. So, training the same set of people to function differently has become a huge part of our everyday lives. Things are changing all the time within our factories. We've made reskilling an inherent part of our organization."

Globally, across about one hundred Flex locations, more than thirty thousand employees have enrolled in the company's Capability Acceleration Program (CAP) to gain new technical and functional skills in domains such as "Surface Mount Technology, Radio Frequency, Mobile, Optics, Plastics, Industrial Engineering, Project Management, Quality, Automation, Supply Chain Management, NPI Test & Test Development, Simulation DES and Extended Reality."[13] The CAP includes offerings for early career employees through senior leaders, covering fundamental, intermediate, and advanced levels. Flex's learning center in Guadalajara, Mexico, has trained more than 1,800 employees since 2023, and a partnership with fourteen colleges and universities in Malaysia delivers continuing education ranging from certificate level to master's degrees, all fully sponsored by the company.

Advaithi noted that such retraining had the added bonus of making Flex more appealing to younger workers. "Back when I started in manufacturing, it really meant standing next to large, greasy machines for ten hours a day. Many assume that's still the environment today, and in some places it is. That vision doesn't appeal to younger generations who have been on their phones or tablets from a young age. But more and more, manufacturing means programming machines and monitoring highly automated production lines. That requires far more technical skills, and in many cases, it can be done from a different location, not standing in front of a machine for ten hours." By optimizing for innovation, Flex can give younger workers a workplace environment more in line with their preferences and more diverse career advancement pathways.

Advaithi has also steered Flex to invest heavily in what she calls "cultural reskilling"—retraining its 130 general managers and factory leaders to embrace truly global collaboration. Traditionally, local executives at any global manufacturer operated in their own silos and defended their independence. But that collection-of-silos model is less and less viable as supply chains become increasingly integrated. "We need to monitor how our Mexico team is working with our Poland team, and how our Poland team is communicating with our Malaysia team. Concentrated manufacturing is changing to more distributed manufacturing. In cases where we used to have customers in just one market, now they're in three different markets, and we might have manufacturing locations in all three."

While Flex's retraining and reskilling is a global imperative, Advaithi is especially passionate about job creation and preservation in the United States, the country that gave her so much opportunity as a young immigrant from India. She's troubled by the decline of some American cities and towns that once offered plenty of well-paying manufacturing jobs. "I want to see small-town America have a resurgence in meaningful jobs. It's one key to overcoming the opioid crisis and other signs of despair. I grew up here and have lived here for the last thirty years, including a lot of time in small manufacturing towns. I have a lot of friends in those communities."

Does this constitute inappropriate favoritism? "Some people might say this committee conflicts with my role as CEO of a global manufacturing company, because I need to make decisions about Flex's workforce in many countries. But I don't hide that one of my priorities is creating jobs in America. I don't make any apologies for it. That priority can coexist with always making decisions in the best interests of Flex. We can create jobs in America and jobs in other countries, too. I don't see it as a zero-sum game. I think it's a good example of how to balance seemingly competing priorities."

This bluntness exemplifies another key to Advaithi's approach to people: her emphasis on consistency. "I don't have the energy or strength to be different people in different settings. I just don't understand people like that. I believe the person who walks in the door at home should be the same person who walks in the door at work."

Graybar: "You Can Be a Real Person and Still Build Confidence"

Like Revathi Advaithi, Kathy Mazzarella runs a company that would probably be more famous if its products and services were a little sexier. She's the chairman, CEO, and president of Graybar, a St. Louis–based Fortune 500 wholesale distributor of electrical, communications, and data networking equipment. Founded in 1869 and employee-owned since 1929, Graybar generates $11 billion in annual revenue and employs 9,500 people in 345 locations across North America, while serving more than 150,000 customers. In 2024, it made *Fortune*'s list of the World's Most Admired Companies for the twenty-second year.[14]

Mazzarella joined Graybar in 1980 and worked her way up to CEO in 2012, so she has participated in a significant share of that impressive history. She believes that a great deal of the company's success stems from its approach to people. She spoke to me about balancing her strength with empathy, warmth, humility, vulnerability—in a word, *humanity*. She intentionally talks to everyone the same way, from frontline workers to her board of directors.

One example of her focus on people and culture: When she became CEO, Mazzarella intentionally tapped Graybar veterans for most senior leadership roles. Only a handful came from outside the company, when she needed expertise in specialized areas. By mostly promoting from within, she was able to maximize institutional knowledge and minimize the chances that a newcomer in a senior role might clash with the organization's collaborative culture.

Still, this type of people-centric leadership isn't easy to maintain consistently. Mazzarella sometimes feels tension between displaying empathy and toughness, between being mindful of people's feelings and holding them accountable for results.

"My brother used to say that I have an iron fist in a soft glove. But especially when somebody is off track or failing, it's important to figure out what's really going on before taking action. It's possible that issues outside of work are affecting their performance, or perhaps the job may not align with their abilities. If you have a private conversation and learn that they are dealing with a personal issue, the right response is: *How can we help you? How can we support you?* But I also think it's possible to be overly empathetic. You still have a business to run, and there are thousands of people depending on your decisions. Often you have to make very difficult decisions, and somebody won't be happy."[15]

One way she stays grounded with her leadership team is by sharing her own challenges, rather than trying to come across as always right. "You can be a real person and still build confidence that you're going to be strong enough to make tough decisions and lead the company through challenges. To me, leadership is about showing your humanity, while also showing your strength." Mazzarella embodies a key principle of Systems Leadership: it's a false choice to think you can be ambitious or kind but not both. "People have always said to me, 'Kathy, you're so driven, you're so ambitious.' But guess what? I still do have a heart."

A big part of empathy is listening to feedback. Mazzarella enjoys employee gatherings where she can talk to people face-to-face and ask them about their concerns. She's happy to meet employees at her office if they request a meeting, because, in her words, "This is their company." She also takes anonymous employee surveys very seriously. "I read all the survey data, all the comments. I'm looking for trends that show where we can do better."

I was especially struck by Mazzarella's humility when describing the arc of her career. "I really am just a normal person who had a wonderful opportunity to find a company that cared about me and that I cared about in return. I was fortunate to find a company that shared my values, where people took care of each other. When people find out that I'm in my forty-fourth year at the same company, they often act like there's something wrong with me. Why did I stay so long? Didn't I ever want another job? I explain that I've had many different jobs here, and I was able to pursue my dreams and feel value and purpose."

Is this notion of long-term loyalty too old-fashioned for Millennial and Gen Z employees, who are stereotyped as job-hopping every eighteen months? Mazzarella doesn't think so. "I find that today's young people want a workplace where they feel valued and feel a sense of community, but they're not sure what that looks like. So as employers, we have to figure out how to give our people the development, the training, and the support they need." A lot of people move on to seek those things, but if they can find them within a well-led organization, their urge to job-hop should be greatly reduced.

Mubadala: "You Have to Connect with People"

On the other side of the world from Advaithi in Austin and Mazzarella in St. Louis, Khaldoon Al Mubarak wrestles with some of the same cross-pressures around developing and leading people. He's the managing director and group CEO of the Mubadala Investment Company, a sovereign wealth fund of the Emirate of Abu Dhabi. It was founded in 2017 from the merger of the Mubadala Development Company and the International Petroleum Investment Company, and has more than $300 billion in assets under management. Mubadala is a global financial powerhouse with 55,000 employees across many subsidiaries. Its mandate is to deliver sustainable returns for its shareholder, the government of Abu Dhabi, and in doing so to develop and advance the United Arab Emirates' knowledge and innovation economy.

Al Mubarak is a Systems Leader who believes passionately that Mubadala's future success depends entirely on hiring, developing, retaining, and learning from the best possible talent. He's been proactive in hiring and promoting young, talented people—both men and women. He stresses the importance of empowering leaders at all levels as a key strategy for retention. He embodies the principle that when you empower employees to make their own decisions instead of telling them what to do, turnover drops and results improve.

At the same time, he finds that he has much less time to spend on his people than he would ideally like. In addition to overseeing Mubadala's vast operations, he holds several prominent positions in the government of Abu Dhabi, and also chairs and serves on the boards of several other significant companies. One that he chairs is the City Football Group (CFG), which owns thirteen football clubs around the world, the most famous of which is Manchester City in the English Premier League. In other words, Al Mubarak has a lot on his plate, even by the standards of a CEO with global operations. As a result, he says, "I don't have the luxury of spending time training people or mentoring as much as I want."[16]

To balance the cross-pressure of his passion for developing people with the demands on his calendar, Al Mubarak finds creative ways to integrate leadership into his other activities. "There are many meetings where I purposely bring in folks from different layers within the organization, unrelated to the business at hand, as a moment of mentoring. Let's say I have a meeting planned with the CEO of a major hedge fund or private equity firm. I might bring a senior C-class executive but also someone else, two or three levels below. I've found that that pays off in building a coaching relationship with that person, as an investment in their future." Al Mubarak will rotate such opportunities among numerous younger executives, soliciting their insights after each meeting while giving them rare access to high-level conversations.

Another way he works coaching into his schedule is by being very intentional about when he will or won't step in to resolve an internal conflict. "There are some issues that can only be addressed and resolved at my level. But there are many more issues that shouldn't be escalated to me. It's important to set a clear definition of where that line is." Al Mubarak doesn't want to overstep his role and make decisions that should be handled by someone else, such as the head of a business unit or local operation. Even if that leader wants to "push this up to Khaldoon," he will usually decline. He wants his executives to practice making hard decisions on their own.

His prioritization isn't merely good for developing new leaders; it's also a survival strategy. "Mubadala is in over fifty countries, many different jurisdictions. We're dealing with a lot of projects, big and small. I try to limit the points where I have to interfere and handle things myself, perhaps by flying to New York or Brazil or Japan or Korea." Flying around the world putting out fires would be both a poor way to show faith in his subordinates and a great way for him to burn out.

Such delegation also aligns with his commitment to trusting experts rather than pretending he knows everything. "I know when one of my executives is far better equipped than me in terms of a specific financial acumen or technical acumen. If that person knows more than me about a particular country or issue, I trust their judgment. I think a leader should think like a generalist most of the time and rely on subject matter experts. While you have good judgment, as a generalist you have to appreciate another's expertise."

Like any Systems Leader, Al Mubarak recognizes the importance of blending IQ and EQ, and knows that some challenges require more empathy than intellectual analysis. "I love individuals who have that balance between IQ and EQ, because it's hard. I cannot tell you that all of my senior executives have that balance. Sometimes you can have the most talented people with extremely high IQ but very weak EQ, which means someone else needs to cover for them in that area." He is willing to put extra time into coaching or covering for those who need help with empathy and emotional intelligence. "It's about knowing your team. I can give you an analysis of my top executives with a high level of confidence. I know what works and what doesn't work with them. I know their strengths and weaknesses. I know exactly what I need to supplement sometimes."

Above all, Al Mubarak believes passionately in forging personal relationships as part of every interaction, to reinforce his humanity and humility. This is especially true within Abu Dhabi, where regular people might be nervous to interact with him. "You have to connect with people. You need to know who you're dealing with, their background, their interests, and find a common touchpoint. In my experience touchpoints are very important, whether it's talking about their family or a mutual interest in football. You have to probe for a real connection."

Leading People Is Most Urgent During Crises and Cycles

Sometimes the need to develop your people will be thrust upon you as an urgent problem, rather than as an initiative that you can ponder, test, and gradually implement on a conservative timeline.

ChatGPT's public launch in November 2022 landed on colleges and high schools like a meteor. Within twenty-four hours, students nationwide were testing what it could do for their homework assignments and papers, while educators began to panic. If a free website could answer almost any question at almost any length in seconds, that would be the end of authentic student writing! Some schools moved quickly to ban the use of AI software entirely. Others began a shift from take-home assignments back to in-class, handwritten essays or oral tests.

On the other hand, some educators took a deep breath before treating this moment as a crisis. That first day I was ready to fight against student laziness and ban the tool in my classes. But then I realized students were going to use it whether I wanted them to do so or not, and I needed to change my strategy. I told them that if they wanted to use ChatGPT on their take-home assignments, I wouldn't stop them. But I would expect two things from them: First, they had to disclose whether their written work included any AI-generated content. Second, any assignment they submitted with the help of AI had to be clearly better than whatever they would have done without it, based solely on my judgment. My thinking was that if ChatGPT made their output better, experimenting with it was worth a try. But if it didn't raise their game, it was just a tool for enabling laziness.

This was hardly a true crisis compared to so many worse things going on in the world. But it was an instructive moment about coping with any unexpected new technology or other sudden change.

It's always tempting to fight disruption, but that never works—the genie can never be put back into the bottle. Instead of resisting change, Systems Leaders try to integrate it into their world by clarifying their true priorities. In this example, ChatGPT might have made my students' writing smoother or faster, but it couldn't actually *think* for them. It couldn't read a case study and respond with *original* insights. It couldn't listen to a guest speaker and analyze how that person's experiences reinforced or contradicted our readings. So, there was no need to panic that American education was doomed. Even after this sudden, shocking change, we could still teach analysis and critical thinking.

All of the people-related issues we've been looking at in this chapter become especially acute during times of crisis, or whenever business cycles turn against a company or industry. Running companies is fun during economic booms, when customers are eager to spend money, markets are growing, and new opportunities abound. Unfortunately, such times never last. Even if there are no sudden disruptions in your industry, economic contractions follow expansions as dependably as sunsets follow sunrises.

Whenever storm clouds gather on the horizon, the most common reaction is to "batten down the hatches" and prepare for an onslaught of volatility and turbulence. For many companies, this tendency manifests itself via budget cuts, killed projects, and often, employee layoffs. Yet those reactions can be just as ineffective (or even counterproductive) as ordering students not to try ChatGPT. For instance, slashing training programs can demoralize staff and trigger a loss of collective competencies that might take years to recover from.

Systems Leaders need to approach these situations, whether triggered by economic cyclicality or an exogenous shock, by holding on to two optimistic thoughts: that difficult times can be survived with careful attention to what's truly important, and that such times never last forever. This means resisting the urge to slash budgets with a meat cleaver during times of duress. Andy Grove used to say frequently that you can't save your way out of a recession—you must invest your way out of a recession. Try to see crises and downturns as opportunities to drive your organization in new directions and to embrace changes that will add value in the future, when good times return.

Similarly, I believe that Systems Leaders need to run into the disruptions in their market, industry, or the entire economy. I think of it much like a first responder or firefighter who runs toward the scene of an accident or into a burning building. The natural human instinct is to run away—to stay safe and not take the risk of getting hurt in a dangerous situation. But if your company or industry is confronting a potentially existential threat, your people will be counting on you to take positive, proactive steps. This may include *expanding* training and developing people rather than balancing your budget at their expense.

When Corie Barry, CEO of Best Buy, visited my class in 2021, she gave us a valuable slogan: "You can't fall in love with how you do business today." She noted that Best Buy's business in 2012, when it faced intense competition from Amazon and Apple, created an opportunity for the company to completely change how it operated. At a time when her family and friends questioned why she would stay with what appeared to be a sinking ship, she acknowledged that no one expected Best Buy to survive. On the other hand, she said, "Being an underdog can be liberating." The only employees who would remain at Best Buy, or join during their crisis, would be those willing to do things completely differently than in the past.

This reminded me of some wisdom I'd gotten at Intel back in

1994, courtesy of cofounder Bob Noyce: "Don't be encumbered by history. Go off and do something wonderful."

The End of an Era?

In April 2024, GE sold the sixty-acre Crotonville campus and its buildings for $22 million. Its new owners planned to turn it into a general-purpose conference center, rentable to any organization that wanted to use it. It was an unremarkable transaction in the world of commercial real estate, but it was a seminal moment in the world of executive education. The days of large, elaborate centers for offsite training were falling out of fashion. Boeing, 3M, and Salesforce have also sold similar facilities in recent years.[17]

Those lamenting the sale included Suzy Welch, Jack's widow and a business writer and educator in her own right. She argued in an essay that it represented "the end of an era: one when companies and employees were on the same team. That's done and over, isn't it? Today, companies and employees are each in a boxer's crouch, glaring across the ring." She continued wistfully: "Crotonville was a shrine to . . . people who so bought into the company's values that they considered it an honor to be invited to an off-site program where they got to talk about those ideas even more than they did at work. Crotonville was based on the notion that you could love your company. And your company could love you."[18]

I don't know if GE or any other company has ever really loved its people. There was a time when I struggled with certain behaviors I saw at Stanford, and one of my colleagues texted me: "When a person loves an institution as much as you love Stanford it never ends well." I replied: "I know that the institution is not capable of loving me, but some of the people in it will. And that's kind of cool."

I also don't think we should romanticize the idea that a company educating (or otherwise supporting) its employees is about love. But I do believe that education creates opportunities for both individuals and organizations to thrive. And whether you do or don't "have a heart" is much less important than seeing the critical need of ensuring that employees are well trained in an increasingly rapidly changing world.

It's up to Systems Leaders to make sure that happens.

Questions to Ponder

- As you read about Crotonville in its heyday, does it seem like a lost paradise of mutual love between employers and employees, as Suzy Welch suggests? Or a relic of an outdated indulgence by large corporations? Or something else?

- Do you agree that "Learning is the new pension"? Or would you rather work for a company that provides generous retirement benefits but no support for your continuing education?

- When you hear that a famously tough-minded company like Amazon is spending more than $1 billion on training, does that strike you as a sincerely generous investment in its people, or a profit-driven move plus some PR spin? Does it matter which motivation is closer to the truth?

- Do you agree with Revathi Advaithi that retraining for modern manufacturing jobs can help relieve the widespread despair in struggling parts of the United States? Is that a valid priority for the CEO of a multinational corporation?

- Do you think that Kathy Mazzarella's forty-four-year (and counting) career at Graybar is impossible to replicate these days? Or is it still possible with the right mindset among both employees and employers?

- Can you resist the temptation to step in and solve problems that really should be on someone else's desk, the way Khaldoon Al Mubarak does?

- Have you ever faced a sudden disruption to your industry, comparable to educators confronting the launch of ChatGPT? Did you and those around you mostly react with anxiety or panic, or by calmly adapting to the new reality?

- What are you and your company doing to facilitate the ongoing retraining and reskilling of your people?

CHAPTER 6

Sphere of Influence:
Internal *and* External

Inside and Outside

When I was at Intel in the 1990s, I spent a few years working in business development, an innovation group that invested in start-ups, explored new product opportunities, and worked on partnerships with large companies. Almost all of our work was done outside headquarters. Cognizant that my team's work was removed from Intel's existing business units, my boss would periodically ask me to embed for a week with one of those units. The goal of these experiences was for me to get a clearer sense of how the unit was doing and also to show its team members the types of innovations and new technologies we were seeing beyond Intel's four walls.

Working for a full week with my Intel colleagues responsible for creating the products that drove Intel's revenue turned out to be a great way to build mutual trust. When they saw that I could actually deliver as an operator—that I wasn't just there to blather on about new technologies but could actually be a useful resource on their tasks—it bolstered my credibility as well as that of our "future-focused" group. My colleagues started to pay closer attention to trends I flagged that might not affect them for a few more years, but that I had seen being developed by startups outside Intel.

Meanwhile, those weeks gave me a granular understanding of the business units' day-to-day and month-to-month challenges, as well as their management dynamics, good or bad. I always went back to my own group with a much fuller picture of how our business units were doing, compared to what we might have learned from the usual updates circulated throughout the corporation.

Nevertheless, I also felt an interesting cross-pressure during those projects—a tension between my obligations to the innovation group and to my teammates in those business units. At my annual reviews, I would be evaluated against metrics set for the innovation group, such as investments made in startups or deep dives into new technologies and markets. Yet a chunk of my time and effort were going to help other parts of the company—units that were essential to driving Intel's revenues, but whose success would not be credited to my own team. At first, I often wondered why my bosses insisted on these forays into our business units, even though they seemed divorced from my group's external-focused goals.

After several years, however, I realized that this arrangement was part of my training as a relatively new executive. Senior management wanted me to understand that to maximize my impact, I couldn't merely focus on the sexy aspects of investing in startups and exploring future markets. I needed my perspective to extend far beyond my group, to Intel's broader ecosystem. My bosses pushed me to engage with the duality of the internal workings of our large company (at that time one of the most valuable on earth) while simultaneously becoming more dialed in to trends and challenges across Silicon Valley and around the world.

In other words, they were helping me navigate the cross-pressure of *sphere of influence*: demands for my attention both internally and externally. As we've seen in our studies of priorities and people, the path to more effective leadership in this dimension is a *both/and* mindset.

Thinking About Your Ever-Changing Ecosystem

Most business leaders prioritize the needs of their customers, employees, and investors, in some combination. But every company also has a broader ecosystem of external players it needs to be constantly considering. This ecosystem includes partners and suppliers, who are usually allies; competitors, who are usually adversaries; and companies that might toggle between acting as partners or competitors in different situations, for whom an appropriate term might be "frenemies." In these scenarios, not all cooperation has been replaced by competition, but a complex interplay fluctuates between the extremes.

Now that alliances shift faster than ever and partners can more easily turn into competitors (think of Uber getting into logistics or Amazon building its own last-mile delivery service), it can be harder than ever to distinguish true friends from frenemies. And it can be even harder to influence those frenemies in whatever direction you want them to turn. One tool that leaders can use in these complex situations is called an "influence map" of the industry. It allows them to sketch out which parts of an ecosystem drive others and to what extent.[1] A well-drawn influence map will include the relative sizes of the players, the nature of their relationships (whether benevolent or adversarial), and the degree of influence they have over each other.

Below is a sample map for UCSF Medical Center, a public hospital system in San Francisco that is part of the University of California. This large organization runs many hospitals and patient care facilities while also serving as a hub of research and teaching in the medical and biological sciences. Its exceptionally complex ecosystem includes government officials at city, state, and federal levels; a wide range of insurance companies; multiple employee unions; private philanthropists who often seek to influence UCSF policy while helping others; many kinds of suppliers; and, of course, patients.

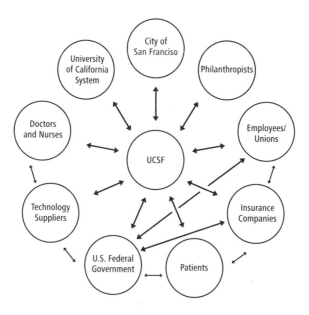

Visualizing these kinds of influences can enable Systems Leaders both to prioritize the stakeholders that most urgently need to be moved in a particular direction and to see where new influences (positive or negative) are likely to arise. Leaders can then devise plans for engaging with each member of the ecosystem, including government regulators if applicable. The effectiveness of these engagements can be tracked by regularly updating the influence map.

Ecosystem members are rarely equal in power or influence. You will need to evaluate their relative levels of dependence in order to calculate how much freedom you have to challenge, contradict, or cut ties with one of your frenemies. Here's how my colleague Robert Burgelman summarizes relationships in terms of high versus low influence and dependence:[2]

		DEPENDENCE	
		Low	High
INFLUENCE	**Low**	You and the other entity are basically **strategically indifferent** to each other. You can partner as equals or walk away with little or no consequence.	You are **strategically subordinate** to the other entity, stuck in a position of defensiveness. Since you really need them, you have to find ways to accommodate their needs.
	High	You are **strategically dominant** over the other entity, with the power to impose your will if you choose to exercise that power.	You and the other entity are **strategically interdependent**, with the potential to become great partners in a stable, long-term ecosystem. You might also wage an evenly matched battle for control of the ecosystem.

Adapted from Robert A. Burgelman, Stanford Graduate School of Business

Systems Leaders generally deploy the most resources toward relationships where they have high influence and where an ecosystem partner has the most potential to help accelerate growth. But this doesn't mean that their focus should be restricted to well-established players. Sometimes a small circle on the influence map, perhaps a new startup, has the potential to make a huge difference to your own company or unit. You can never assume that last year's influence map is still accurate, let alone one from five years ago that still lives in your head as representing "the way things are." You may need to redirect most of your resources and incentives toward smaller players who weren't even visible on previous versions of your ecosystem's map.

The more nimble you can be in adjusting your approach to allies, adversaries, and frenemies, the more likely that you will minimize threats and maximize opportunities for growth. Analyzing, monitoring, and trying to organize your ecosystem can be a key component of your long-term success.

Sounds a bit abstract? Let's look at an industry we all rely on—smartphones—to give you a more concrete idea of navigating relationships within an ecosystem.

Android: Navigating an Often Hostile Ecosystem

When Google launched the Android operating system for smartphones in 2008 (after acquiring the startup that developed it), the tech giant took the opposite approach from Apple's closed iOS for its new iPhone. Rather than jealously guarding a proprietary smartphone OS, Google gave Android away to anyone who wanted to build devices with it.

That strategy paid off better than anyone predicted. Android became the OS for over 3 *billion* smartphones, tablets, and other mobile devices worldwide, made by about 1,300 original equipment manufacturers (OEMs), with a global market share north of 70 percent. Google invests billions each year to constantly improve

Android and expand it into new uses, such as smart watches, smart speakers, and automobile operating systems.

In its earnings reports, the company combines revenue from multiple sources (Android, Chrome, Maps, and hardware such as Pixel and Nest devices) under the subheading "Google Services." This makes it hard to tease out the specific revenue generated by Android, but in the first quarter of 2022, this "services" division brought in $6.8 billion, which equates to more than $27 billion per year.[3] Keep in mind that the highly profitable Google Play app store wouldn't exist without Android, and that Google Maps and Google Pay both generate much if not most of their revenue from Android devices.

But even with a dominant global share of mobile OS, Android still faces enormous challenges because of the extreme complexity of its ecosystem. Just consider the many entities on its influence map:

- About 1,300 OEMs worldwide, who have the option to drop Android if they find a better alternative or become disgruntled with its terms of service.

- Thousands of app developers, whose efforts are essential to stocking the Google Play app store.

- Hundreds of cellular carriers around the world, who have the power to disrupt the mobile market with a change in their policies.

- Automakers who may or may not embrace the Android Auto phone-to-screen projection system, which competes with Apple's CarPlay.

- Government regulators in every country, some of whom are on high alert for any predatory abuses of Android's massive market share.

Relying heavily on external partners gave Android many advantages. One was that OEMs in each country were free to customize Android to fit the specific needs of their customers, leading to a wide range of devices—from minimalist and cheap to fully loaded with features and premium priced. Another was that Android's direct marketing expenses were significantly lower than Apple's for the iPhone, because Android's OEM and wireless carrier partners already spent billions to market their products.

On the downside, however, this model took most aspects of quality control out of Google's hands. If an OEM partner produced an inferior product, research showed that many consumers blamed Android rather than the OEM. It was hard if not impossible to ensure consistent user experiences. Even worse, any OEM partner could transform into a direct competitor at any moment. For at least a decade, two of Android's biggest OEMs—Samsung and Amazon, for its Fire phones and tablets—made attempts to replace Android with their own proprietary OS.

In the face of such threats, Android focused on continuing to drive innovation. For instance, in 2014 they launched a slimmed-down OS version for the Indian market, where hundreds of millions of customers wanted smartphones but couldn't afford high-end models. By coordinating new specs with Indian OEMs and embracing mobile advertising as a revenue source, Google helped its partners develop smartphones that could be sold for as little as $100. By 2019, more than 500 million Indians had one, and 74 percent of those were made by a local partner of Android.[4]

Meanwhile, pursuing what CEO Sundar Pichai called "the intersection of hardware and software," Google developed its own smartphone brand, the Pixel, which gave the company full control over a high-end user experience. Launched in 2016, Pixels came with a pure version of Android, with full optimization of all available features.[5] But this move turned Google into a direct competitor to its OEM partners. On Google's org chart, Android and Pixel were siloed units with separate leadership, but to the rest of the ecosystem they both were perceived as simply "Google." As former Android director of product management Sagar Kamdar put it, "We of course want Pixel to be differentiated, but now that we're our own OEM, our partners are asking: How do you think about us relative to your own hardware products? So it's a balancing act for sure."[6]

Google established a communications firewall between the Android and Pixel teams, aiming to reassure frenemies like Samsung and Amazon that Pixel wasn't benefiting from favoritism from the Android team. If anything, the firewall made day-to-day collaboration with Android *harder* for the Pixel team than it was for other OEMs. In April 2024, Google finally gave up on the firewall and reorganized both Android and Pixel as part of a new Platforms and Devices unit, with the goal of faster integration of AI across all products.[7]

Another major threat has been government regulators around the world. In 2018, the European Union's antitrust commission fined Google $5.1 billion for alleged anticompetitive practices related to Android. The EU demanded that Google decouple certain proprietary apps that it preloaded onto Android devices, giving those apps an unfair advantage.[8] Google pushed back both in courts of law and in the court of public opinion, stressing that it did not require any OEMs to include, promote, or favor its apps or services. To this day, the Android website includes a detailed list of facts about how the OS supports fair competition across the entire mobile industry.[9]

Perhaps the key takeaway from Android's history is that the more complex your influence map, the less you can ever relax in your success, and the more fluid and frequent the adaptations you will have to make to both internal and external forces.

Wells Fargo: "It Felt Like We Were in a War"

Another company whose regulators loom large on its influence map is Wells Fargo. In chapter 1 we saw that Charlie Scharf, CEO since 2019, faced tough cross-pressures in his sphere of influence, a legacy of past company practices. Those practices had triggered multiple government investigations and enforcement actions, which led regulators to insist on significant changes in management. Many of the company's managers and employees were demoralized and angry that Wells Fargo had careened so badly off the rails, and that those responsible for protecting and leading the company had failed. The workplace culture suffered immensely.

As Scharf told me, "When I got here, it was very important that everyone understood the gravity of the situation. It felt like we were in a war, not business as usual. Then, during COVID we went from earning $20 billion a year to $4 billion a year. And therefore we needed to make serious changes in the organization."[10] Those changes needed to begin with stabilizing basic operations. Scharf was mindful of what Lou Gerstner had said years earlier, when he took over IBM during a crisis: "The last thing IBM needs right now is a vision."[11]

"Wells Fargo had one of the greatest combinations of franchises in financial services. To turn things around, we didn't need a new strategy. We needed strong execution, including solving all of our regulatory issues," Scharf explained. "If we didn't immediately begin to build better operational capabilities and safeguards, it wouldn't matter what strategy or innovations we pursued." With that in mind, Scharf began thinking beyond the company's internal metrics. He stressed in his first letter to shareholders that it was essential to respect their regulators, the communities where they did business, and other stakeholders. "In our industry especially, confidence and reputation really do matter. You can't just run an advertising campaign saying that you're a great company."

But interacting with federal regulators isn't easy, because they have their own unique set of incentives and pressures, and they aren't monolithic. Some are nonpartisan career professionals who believe in the rules and are sincerely committed to enforcing them. Others, closer to the top of each federal agency, are political appointees who may have other agendas beyond simple enforcement. For instance, they might prioritize making themselves and their allies look good, especially in the context of an upcoming election. Any business leader under regulatory scrutiny needs to be mindful of both types of regulators and what it will take to satisfy them.

Scharf told his team that there was no point in complaining about intense regulatory scrutiny. It was simply the new environment they had to accept and adapt to. "They are the judge, the jury, the appellate court, and the Supreme Court. You have to design the organization for the reality at that point in time, not what you theoretically believe is the right thing."

Scharf understood that regulators and legislators are people with emotions, just like everyone else. When some members of the previous Wells Fargo team acted improperly, its regulators were embarrassed by their own failure to catch the problems sooner. "Critics said the government was asleep at the wheel. That wasn't fair to these people, since they didn't commit the fraud." Fair or not, regulators and the relevant Congressional committees never wanted to be in that position again, and part of Scharf's new job was reassuring them that Wells Fargo was now playing by the rules and no threat to anyone.

Managing this position often required more emotional intelligence than financial acumen. Even several years later, Scharf felt this pressure. "It's rare for a week to go by when we don't get some call from a regulator or legislator. But we're building the company back financially in part because we're rebuilding relationships with regulators and legislators."

Reassuring these stakeholders even extended to easing government skepticism of new initiatives that were perfectly legal. As Scharf observed, "It's a funny position to be in, when you're afraid to talk about doing something new and fresh that makes you a bigger, stronger company. Legislators and regulators don't really want us to be a better competitor against small banks or even non-banks like PayPal." Still, innovation couldn't be put on the back burner. "If the world is moving and we're not, we will just create a problem for us tomorrow. So we have to move forward."

Meanwhile, Scharf estimates that he spends 70 percent of his time on the other half of his sphere of influence, inside the company. Restoring morale after a long stretch of cultural dysfunction might be one of the hardest tasks for any new leader. As he put it, "You really don't know what is going on inside until you get the job." His main advice for leaders is to simplify your key talking points and overcommunicate them relentlessly.

Scharf's top message for Wells Fargo's 200,000-plus employees was that even though the company was "in a war," they had an opportunity to build a brighter future together. Starting from rock bottom—badly underperforming and in trouble with the government—they had nowhere to go but up. They just had to remember that they were all in this together, and that the company's critics and competitors, from Wall Street to crypto startups that wanted to tear down the entire financial system, were all outside the building. He also echoed the Nick Saban advice that we discussed earlier—the importance of explaining *why* you were asking people to do things in new ways. And he encouraged people to push back and even to make fun of him sometimes, to reinforce his humanity.

As long as the regulatory leash on the company remains short and tight, so will the pressure to focus both externally and internally. Scharf fully accepts that pressure, even if he wishes he didn't have to.

The University of Montana: Many Stakeholders, One Mission

For a very different kind of ecosystem than Wells Fargo's, consider what Seth Bodnar faces as president of the University of Montana (UM), the state's flagship public university. He spoke to my class in April 2020, soon after COVID forced students and faculty to flee their campuses and adapt to online learning. I was impressed by his empathy for how the crisis was affecting everyone and his determination to lead the university through tough times with minimal damage. But he didn't talk merely about the challenges of that unique moment; he focused on UM's deeper purpose and its essential role in serving a wide range of constituents, including the general public.

Unlike most university presidents, who spend most or all of their careers in academia, Bodnar came to the role in 2018 after distinguished achievements in the military and corporate spheres. He graduated first in his class at West Point, served as an officer in the U.S. Army's 101st Airborne Division and the elite Green Berets, and earned two master's degrees from Oxford. After two years teaching economics at West Point, he began a six-and-a-half-year stint at General Electric.[12]

This exceptional breadth of experience allowed Bodnar to see UM's complex ecosystem with an outsider's perspective. His constituencies include students, their families, faculty, administrators, staff, alumni, and both federal and state regulators. On any given issue, such as admissions and financial aid policies, they might all have conflicting interests. But Bodnar balances those cross-pressures by focusing on UM's core mission: enabling what he calls "inclusive prosperity" for students of various socioeconomic classes by preparing them for careers that are both "ready for today and also tomorrow-proof."[13]

Like other Systems Leaders, Bodnar runs *toward* disruption, whether in the form of a new technology like AI or new admissions rules imposed by the Supreme Court. His mantra during crises is that leaders must hold two truths at the same time: Things can always get worse, yet every challenge creates huge opportunities. Being able to act on both can make the difference between merely surviving a crisis and emerging stronger on the other side.

In a small state like Montana (population 1.13 million), a flagship public university plays a much bigger role than simply educating students. It's an engine for driving the statewide economy and supporting employers that have ties to the university. UM can also be a magnet drawing new companies and jobs into the state, as well as good students across the country who may evolve into future Montanans. Likewise, the university's reputation affects how many of the state's brightest teens choose to remain in Montana, rather than leaving for college and perhaps never returning.

The prominence of his job has made Bodnar a local celebrity, to his surprise. He recalled sheepishly that strangers often greeted him when he was out with his family, or even whispered to each other while gesturing at him. They were all his stakeholders, because everything he did at the university had repercussions far beyond its gates.

Brightline: "Storytelling Is a Critical Leadership Skill"

The healthcare industry may have an even more complex ecosystem than higher education, encompassing many kinds of medical professionals, insurance companies, government payers, federal and state regulators, and customers—i.e., patients and their families. Inside versus outside cross-pressures can get especially tricky for healthcare startups with innovative business models, such as Brightline, which was founded in 2019 in Silicon Valley.

Before COVID made online medical consultations fairly routine, Brightline's innovation was offering kids and teens faster and easier access to professional help, often at lower costs than traditional in-person therapy. The pitch to parents was simple: "whether it's virtual therapy, psychiatry, or coaching," Brightline could help get families support fast.[14] Members could access the company's network of therapists, prescribers, and coaches without long waiting lists, or even chat with experts online within minutes.

Cofounder and CEO Naomi Allen cares deeply about expanding high-quality behavioral health support for every child and teen who needs it. That mission is front and center whenever Allen is recruiting new talent, motivating employees, or raising additional capital. She's also passionate about helping families navigate the often-baffling maze of insurance coverage, which can make it hard to figure out what kinds of treatments are or aren't covered under a given plan. Parents can also face frustrating red tape from school administrators when their kids need behavioral support, and Brightline helps with that challenge, too.

As Allen told me proudly, "Four years ago, few thought pediatric mental health mattered. And here we are with five million members who have access to Brightline. That is a monumental shift in terms of access to mental health. A good 700,000 of those are uninsured, and normally people who do not have health insurance are unable to pay for therapy. So we're literally saving lives. We're healing anxiety and depression and preventing suicides. That's critical for telling the story of our company—for inspiring and engaging and aligning people around what really matters."[15]

But even though she's mission driven, Allen is also a hard-headed Systems Leader. Brightline is not a charity; her investors expect growth and profitability. If the financials don't work, the startup won't survive. That's why, during the broad pullback in venture capital investments in late 2022, she was one of the first startup CEOs to cut her burn rate and pivot from rapid growth toward sustainability—even though Brightline had plenty of cash after a $115 million round of funding. But this belt tightening didn't equate to treating employees badly. When Brightline had to conduct layoffs to reduce that burn rate, Allen made sure the startup was generous toward those let go.

Allen developed her talent for navigating complex ecosystems—for seeing how a wide range of pieces fit together—as a young consultant for McKinsey & Co. She believes in experimenting with new approaches and testing them as objectively as possible, rather than accepting any conventional wisdom uncritically. "One thing we do is what I call a clean sheet exercise. If we were going to relaunch a product or service from scratch, what would we want it to look like, knowing what we know now? Then we ask what it would take to run the business that way, starting from where we are." This approach requires accepting the sunk costs of abandoning old approaches and expectations.

Business professors Wesley M. Cohen and Daniel A. Levinthal have called the ability to embrace new ideas from outside the "absorptive capacity of the organization." They argued that leaders tend to conflate two distinct skills: scanning the outside world for new ideas and data, and then implementing changes within their organization based on that new knowledge. Many leaders focus on the first part, reading widely and going to conferences to absorb the latest trends, insights, and research. But the harder challenge is communicating such ideas from their own brains to their entire organizations, in ways that prompt real and lasting changes.[16] This lines up with my own observation that many leaders find it easier to talk about innovation than also doing the next step of applying it within their own domain.

Naomi Allen is an exception, constantly scanning her broad ecosystem for ideas that she can introduce at Brightline. This requires frequent toggling between her internal and external modes of operating. "There are phases where I've got to be more internally focused and phases where I've got to be more externally focused. I try to step back on a regular cadence, nearly every week, to ask myself if I'm spending my time the right way. Does every meeting on my calendar have to be there? Am I blocking enough time for higher level strategic work?"

Allen doesn't see herself as a naturally internal or external person; she has worked on honing both skillsets. "Right now, for example, because of a new commercial strategy we're trying to put in place, I'm mostly out in the field. I'm interviewing new candidates, talking to new partners, meeting with customers. We're trying to launch a different go-to-market engine, so I've got to have customer input and feedback and alignment around that, as well as partnership input and feedback and alignment. On the other hand, when our growth was going through the roof, my focus was internal. I had to figure out who were our top fifty people that we couldn't afford to lose, so I could have coffee with them. I said, let's get plans in place to retain key performers. Let's make sure we're partnering with our board in terms of an equity refresh."

She talked about getting personally involved with complex strategic renegotiations of key contracts, potentially breaking up with underperforming partner organizations while working to improve results for their key partners. "So there's a lot of commercial strategy and operations that I'm in the weeds on right now." Meanwhile her board wanted Brightline to actively pursue potential acquisi-

SPHERE OF INFLUENCE: INTERNAL *AND* EXTERNAL ■ 137

tions, a classic external endeavor. "That is a very real trade-off right now around how I spend my time."

Allen sees much of her role, both internally and externally, under the umbrella of sales. "Any CEO is selling to investors, partners, new hires, customers. Selling your vision to employees and getting them aligned around expectations. Convincing them that those expectations are also good for their careers." Especially at a privately held startup, communicating and aligning with the board, which includes major investors, is essential. Allen works closely on that sphere of influence with her CFO and executive team.

She is constantly working to become a better storyteller to complement her more analytical, problem-solving nature. "I admire people who are good communicators at the 20,000-foot level, putting a company's achievements into historical context. Those who can show the arc of their impact or mission in simple terms. Especially in health care, people hunger for clear impact, such as 'saving a million lives from diabetes.' So, I think storytelling is a critical leadership skill. It's worth the time to step away from operations and the day-to-day demands on your calendar to generate those stories and make those connections between your business strategy and your mission."

Allen acknowledges that there are still some successful companies where senior management still follows the model of an externally focused CEO and an internally focused COO, so they can divide and conquer both spheres of influence. "I worked for a CEO like that—Glen Tullman, who ran Livongo. He was sales driven and really great at telling the company's story and rallying the team. He also had a president and COO who ran everything internally, and other strong internal leaders." But she agrees that developing both skillsets is more important than ever for aspiring leaders.

"Perhaps my least favorite aspect of this job is being expected to wear different faces for different internal and external conversations. . . . I don't like to shade my comments or answers to any audience. I'd like to say whatever I'm going to say regardless of who's in the room. But that's almost antithetical to the job. So one of the hardest things for me as a leader is pausing to ask myself, is this appropriate for this audience, or not?"

That's the flip side of what Revathi Advaithi said about being the same person no matter what room she walks into. You can have the integrity to be the same person while still being purposeful about how you frame messages differently in different rooms.

Box: "I Consider It a False Choice"

Aaron Levie is cofounder and CEO of the enterprise cloud services company Box, and one of the Systems Leaders I most admire in Silicon Valley. I got to know him well when we jointly taught a Stanford class on "The Industrialist's Dilemma" for five years. He's intellectually deep, thoughtful, and emotionally intelligent, and he perseveres through tough times in an unforgiving B2B industry.

While many of Box's competitors in cloud computing and enterprise content management (ECM) have struggled in recent years, Box's results are still moving up and to the right. Part of that success is driven by Levie's commitment to constant reinvention. As *TechCrunch* noted in 2024, "Levie has always had a knack for seeing where the puck is going, and his company is embracing the software shift toward AI and workflow automation."[17] It's been an eventful two decades since he started the company in his dorm room at USC.

Levie finds his greatest satisfaction neither in big-picture strategizing nor in "make the trains run on time" operations, but in hands-on product development. As he put it, "I choose to do what

I do because it's the only reason I wanted to do startups in the first place. I didn't get into startups for operational drudgery or for 30,000-foot-high strategy. I love the details of product. That's where the rubber meets the road in our kind of business."[18]

Levie means no disrespect to leaders whose greatest strength is strategy or operations. "I don't think my particular approach is a template for everyone, but it works for me. Tim Cook has obviously brought a much more operational bent to Apple and he's been insanely successful, just as Steve Jobs was as a strategist. But my closest role model is probably Satya Nadella. He's an incredible product guy, laser focused on figuring out the next product category that Microsoft needs to pursue, then unleashing his world-class team of operators to make it happen."

Levie doesn't even see his ecosystem in terms of internal and external spheres of influence; he thinks that's an arbitrary and unnecessary distinction, at least for his kind of software. "I consider it a false choice. To me, our corporate partners are essentially internal, because we build software that by definition has to connect to them. They are just as crucial as anyone within Box. Our partners help us deliver our product, and our customers pay the bills. For us the border between inside and outside is very porous."

In his relentless quest for useful feedback, Levie devotes about 40 to 50 percent of his time to external work, sometimes more. "My biggest priority is spending time with customers. They are the unending lifeblood of valuable information about what we should do differently, what we should build next, and how we should price our products. I'm always trying to get as much information as possible from customers." But he stresses that this kind of external work feeds directly into his relations with the people who work inside Box. Deeper understanding of customers drives better leadership of product development, strategy, and operations alike. Many startups talk about "product-market fit," but Levie thinks in terms of "product-founder-customer fit"—with his role serving as a critical connecting point.

Of course, no matter how much he'd like to focus all his attention on products and customers, Levie still has to wrestle with strategy and operations, and he agrees that today's leaders need to hone their skills at all of the above. "Our greatest source of tension is probably that we have to grow, *and* we have to be profitable. It was far more straightforward when we only had to grow. And it could be very straightforward if we only had to be profitable. But we face the tension of allocating our resources and energy toward both goals, with a bunch of constraints in the system. That's one of the most intellectually fun parts of my job, but also one of the hardest. We have to have high conviction about our product bets and the market opportunities we're going after. That's where the squeeze comes from."

Questions to Ponder

- Do you have "frenemy" relationships in your industry? How challenging have they been to navigate?

- Can you draw an influence map to visualize all the players in your ecosystem and their mutual relationships?

- Do you think Google made a mistake in creating its Pixel unit to build its own devices using the Android operating system, thus competing directly with its huge global network of OEM partners?

- Do you agree with Charlie Scharf about the importance of simplifying your key talking points and over-communicating them relentlessly? Or would that leadership approach risk making your people feel infantilized?

- As of early-2025, American colleges and universities are facing a record number of presidential vacancies. Do you think Seth Bodnar's success suggests that they should be more open to people with military and business leadership backgrounds, rather than purely academic expertise? Why or why not?

- Naomi Allen spoke of the upside of the old model of "divide and conquer" leadership, in which executives could thrive with a reputation as purely inside or outside leaders. Do you prefer that to the Systems Leadership model of embracing both roles equally? Why?

- Do you agree with Aaron Levie that dividing a leader's spheres of influence into internal and external is an arbitrary distinction? Or do you find this conceptual framework helpful in thinking about leadership challenges?

CHAPTER 7

Geography:
Local *and* Global

Oversimplified at Best, Wildly Inaccurate at Worst

I first visited the Kingdom of Saudi Arabia with a group of Stanford students in 2017. Before that trip, our group studied the history of the country and received advice about local customs. Nevertheless, I was slightly afraid as my wife and I headed to the San Francisco airport. Would an Islamic theocracy really welcome an American teacher whose last name is Siegel? What would happen when we encountered Saudi citizens, business leaders, and government officials? After teaching many Saudi students over the years, some of whom had evolved into close friends, I wanted to see their homeland with my own eyes. But I didn't really know what we'd experience in a country whose culture seemed utterly alien.

I could not have been more surprised by what we actually found in Riyadh. Everyone we met was kind, friendly, open-minded, and hospitable. They were excited about the stirrings of dramatic changes in their society and the chance to engage more fully and equally with the rest of the world. At several meetings I had with Saudi companies on behalf of my venture fund, the discussion topics were the same as at meetings in Chicago, Munich, or Shanghai. Everyone shared the same types of challenges that trouble leaders worldwide, especially how to foster innovation and battle against bureaucracy. They were eager to share the history of their country and talk about ways they were planning to improve Saudi Arabia's entrepreneurship, innovation, venture capital, and business education.

In retrospect, I should have suspected as much before my arrival in Riyadh. I already knew from experience that one should never rely on stereotypes or punditry to form opinions about a place. Every preconception I had brought on my first trips to countries in Europe, Asia, and Latin America turned out to be oversimplified at best or wildly inaccurate at worst. Every culture has nuances, and even if you read broadly and deeply in advance, you can't really know a country until you spend significant time there. Why did I assume Saudi Arabia would be any different? At the end of that first trip, I realized that I had learned so much yet still knew so little.

I made several more trips there over the next few years for business and teaching opportunities. By the time one of my former students invited me to a 2022 dinner with several Stanford alumni, I could honestly say that I had never seen a country change so much in just five years. The business and government officials at that dinner, several of whom were my former students, engaged thoughtfully and enthusiastically about the opportunities and challenges Saudi Arabia faced as it began to reduce its dependence on extracting and exporting oil. They envisioned a modern, diverse economy that would be more tightly integrated into a wide range of global industries.

The next evening I had another dinner with a group of young Saudi investors, entrepreneurs, and government employees who were also overflowing with optimism. They, too, believed their country was on a path to a new era of opportunity and growth, with much less tension with the West and a much broader economy.

The New York Times wrote in 2024 about the government's attempts to boost tourism by changing the old stereotypes: "Long associated with Islamic extremism, human rights abuses and the oppression of women, the kingdom has made strides in recent years to refashion its society and its reputation abroad."[1] Among the examples were reduced or abandoned restrictions on clothing, public concerts, and the freedom of women to drive and to travel unaccompanied. Clearly, the world was noticing Saudi Arabia's concerted effort to become a more comfortable place for Westerners to visit and do business.

My surprising experiences there parallel those of others who've spent time in countries that most people know only by stereotypes, from China to Brazil to India to the United States. All are complex and changing constantly. But how are business leaders supposed to deal with so much global diversity and complexity? No one can spend quality time in all 195 countries.* We have to depend on secondhand information, but how can we know which sources are trustworthy?

This dilemma goes to the heart of today's leadership cross-pressure around geography. On one hand, today's global economy offers tremendous opportunities, not merely for manufacturing and supply chains but also for driving massive worldwide demand for goods and services. You may recall the shorthand I introduced in chapter 1: "Globalization 1.0" refers to the mostly supply-side era of the late twentieth century, when low-cost manufacturing and customer service in Asia and elsewhere offered huge cost savings to Western businesses. In contrast, I call our current era "Globalization 2.0" because it adds more opportunities to find customers as well as workers in distant parts of the world, by enabling independent centers of excellence and innovation rather than a strict hub-and-spoke organizational model with a single global headquarters.

On the other hand, each opportunity created by globalization comes with potential pitfalls and risks. During Globalization 1.0, many politicians underestimated the negative consequences of widespread displacement of labor and capital, including a rise in anger-driven populism everywhere from the United States to Brazil to France. Western leaders failed to anticipate the corrosive damage to many communities when manufacturing jobs moved to low-wage countries, as well as how important it would be to retrain factory workers for new jobs. Had more attention and planning been applied to those communities, the last few decades might have played out very differently. We're only recently beginning to see

---

* Give or take a few, depending on how you define a country.

some counter-trends, with an upsurge in manufacturing jobs in U.S. states such as South Carolina, where European and Asian automakers have built new factories. By building cars closer to their ultimate customers and boosting goodwill with the American public via job creation, such automakers create win-win outcomes. During Globalization 2.0, the pursuit of cheap labor is merely one of many interests that leaders must consider.

Regardless of how one feels about such trends, few businesses have the option of ignoring globalization altogether. It's getting harder and harder to lead any kind of company, of any size, with a strictly local mindset on either the supply side or the demand side. As much as we might fantasize about economic independence (at the level of either companies or countries), the global economy becomes more interdependent every year.

As a Systems Leader, you will almost certainly be crossing borders more and more in the future, either physically or virtually. So you must learn to think and act both locally and globally at the same time, whether you produce and distribute physical products or intangibles like software, entertainment, or financial services. While you can't visit every country—or even every country where you do business—you can become more open-minded about gathering information. You can push beyond your usual media bubble and comfort zone. And you can get better at seeing the bigger picture of interconnected global systems.

The examples in this chapter will show you how Systems Leaders are accomplishing all of the above.

So Similar Yet So Different

In early 2020, COVID prompted me to convert my home office into a remote teaching studio, with a high-quality 4K camera, professional lighting, and multiple screens so I could see the faces of dozens of students while controlling my slides and other graphics. Suddenly, instead of going out into the world, the world was able to come right inside my home office. That studio has remained enormously useful, long after in-person meetings and conferences resumed.

On one memorable day a few years ago, I started my morning teaching a group of executives from Oman in my home office. Right after that session I drove to the Stanford campus and taught a group of graduate students in the classroom. I then met with another group of students over lunch, followed by meetings with colleagues and administrators in the afternoon. At 5 PM I went back to my home studio for a Zoom with a group of entrepreneurs in South Korea. That was followed by a dinner back on campus with students. Then I drove home one last time and squeezed in a 10 PM speech to a group of executives in Malaysia before bed. When I finally logged off, I realized that I had spent the day teaching leaders in four very different countries, thousands of miles apart, without physically leaving a five-mile radius. That would have been unthinkable just a decade earlier.

The variety of that day was highlighted by the cultural differences and diverse national interests that shape the business communities in Oman, Malaysia, South Korea, and the United States. Two of the groups I addressed worked for sovereign energy and telecommunication companies, which don't even exist in the United States. Each of the four governments has a different level of regulation and entanglement with their business communities. Thus, as similar as those audiences were in many respects, they required a subtle understanding of their unique attributes and situations.

It wasn't so long ago (at least from my Gen X perspective) that global geopolitics seemed straightforward. The NATO countries,

Japan, the Asian Tigers, and their allies represented democratic capitalism. The Soviet Union, China, and their allies represented authoritarian communism. These two large blocs competed for influence everywhere else, and business leaders in each country faced strong pressure to support their own government and its allies.

The relative stability of the Cold War ended with the collapse of the USSR, turning a bipolar world into a far more complex multipolar world. Now, thirty-five years after the fall of the Berlin Wall, we still have many countries that embrace either democratic capitalism or authoritarian communism. But we also have China and others representing "dictatorial capitalism"—in which a communist government uses private companies to advance its geopolitical goals. We have parts of Europe blurring the lines between welfare state capitalism and democratic socialism. We have Russia dominated by a business oligarchy and a quasidemocracy, in which the president won his fifth term in 2024 with a suspiciously high 88 percent of the vote. And that's just scratching the surface of the variety of environments in which today's leaders conduct international business.

More Sources of Global Complexity

Meanwhile, all this diversification in economic governance since the 1990s has been accompanied by other trends and crises that have further reshaped global commerce—with, in many cases, international governments becoming even more intertwined with business, presenting leaders with new challenges.

The Global Financial Crisis of 2008–9 prompted governments around the world to inject massive amounts of capital into the financial industry to prevent a collapse of the world's monetary systems. Banks, insurers, and other financial firms accepted increased oversight and regulation in exchange for huge bailouts that allowed them to stay in business. Some of the world's largest companies had to restructure their governance and capital ratios, leading to massive changes in how they operated.

A decade later, the COVID pandemic of 2020–21 further intertwined governments with the private sector. When societies around the world shut down in March 2020, devastating industries such as aviation, hospitality, and tourism, massive injections of capital into the global economy followed. With direct cash disbursements to citizens, and forgivable loans to enterprises of all sizes, the notion of a laissez-faire economy became quaintly outdated. The sheer size of global government intervention was staggering. One report showed that governments allocated $10 trillion to economic stimulus in the first two months of the pandemic, nearly *ten times more* than what they had spent during the 2008–9 crisis.[2] Interest rates were lowered to zero, or even to negative levels in some cases, further reinforcing unprecedented government action and engagement in the global economy.

Nor should we underplay the impact of increasing economic espionage and international cybercrime. By some estimates, over 40 percent of cyberattacks against businesses are driven by governments, not organized crime.[3] That might even be an underestimate, as some countries turn to criminal proxies to conceal their efforts.[4] Businesses of all sizes must now be constantly vigilant against hackers trying to steal confidential information or get access to their customers' private data. And cybersecurity must include not just sophisticated technical defenses but also diplomatic engagement with governments, who might be turning a blind eye (or worse) to hackers based in their countries.

Finally, as I noted in chapter 2, leaders need to make hard choices about whether they will do business in countries whose policies they find offensive or alarming. Such cases are rarely black-and-white, and we'll meet Systems Leaders who approach similar dilemmas very differently. My goal in the rest of this chapter is not to tell you whether or not to engage with certain countries but to show a range of strategies that can be applied now that businesses and governments are more inexorably intertwined than ever before. Wherever you may land on a given issue (such as labor conditions, climate impact, gender inequality, or LGBTQ rights), you won't have the luxury of simply refusing to engage with certain countries without understanding the consequences of such decisions on your employees, customers, and other stakeholders.

Nike: "Of China and for China"

John Donahoe became president and CEO of Nike in January 2020, after a wide-ranging career that included nearly two decades at Bain & Company and stints as CEO of ServiceNow and eBay.[5] Just as he was settling into his new job, Nike had to confront massive production and supply chain disruptions caused by COVID. That was the start of an extremely challenging four-year stretch, during which the company faced innovative new competitors such as Hoka and On, along with traditional rivals such as Adidas. The perception spread that Nike was falling behind on innovation, especially in its largest product category of running gear. Meanwhile, the company was finding it hard to replace aging superstar endorsers like Tiger Woods.[6] It all added up to significant declines in market share and profit margins, especially as inflationary pressures raised production costs.

As part of his response, Donahoe focused on pivoting the company toward direct consumer sales and relying less on traditional retail middlemen. As *Business Insider* noted, "It could help the iconic marketing company control every aspect of how its customers buy shoes, from the first advertisement to the final purchase. At the same time, Nike would have the essential data it needs to understand its shoppers on a deeper level."[7] The *Financial Times* praised his initial comeback plan: "Donahoe has moved quickly to make changes" with "one of the largest overhauls in the company's history, eschewing Nike's internal organization by sport categories—such as running, basketball and football—in favor of silos for men, women and kids."[8]

When Donahoe visited my class in April 2024, I was impressed by his focus on listening more closely to the athletes who were still Nike's core customers; on acknowledging and fixing past mistakes; on learning from upstart competitors rather than dismissing them; and on prioritizing people and culture even ahead of strategy and execution. In other words, he spoke like a Systems Leader.

Donahoe was particularly forceful when he discussed Nike's complex relationship with China. Some activists called for corporate disinvestment to pressure the Chinese government, but Nike was unmoved. In response to a question from an analyst in 2021, Donahoe said: "Nike is a brand that is of China and for China . . . We have been in China for over 40 years."[9] As he told my class, Nike will speak out publicly on international issues when directly relevant to their business, and they work hard to make sure their global partners engage in legal and humane labor practices. But otherwise, he is not inclined to publicly comment on other cultures or governments.

While Nike manufactures many of its shoes and clothes throughout Asia, including in Vietnam and Indonesia, China is increasingly important on the demand side as well. In fact, China generates about 20 percent of Nike's global consumer revenue, making it their third-biggest market. Young people in China want to wear cool sneakers and clothes worn by cool global superstars—just like their peers around the world.

As Donahoe told CNBC in 2023, during a period of rising U.S.-China tensions: "If you're a global company, you've got to just accept that and try to steer a course that is consistent with your strategy and consistent with your values. . . . We very much understand ourselves to be a local citizen with our China consumers and our China team. We're trying to maintain a long-term view."[10]

In his defense, Nike sells shoes and T-shirts, not military technology. At best, Donahoe's pro-China stance helped build bridges between two of the world's superpowers; at worst, it was of little relevance to America's national security. When he told CNBC that Nike was "of China and for China," I assume his intended audience was Beijing, not Wall Street or Washington, DC. Donahoe knew very well that deep in its DNA, Nike is still of Beaverton, Oregon.

In September 2024, with Nike still suffering from slow growth, disappointing results from its direct e-commerce initiatives, and the challenges of turning around the organization, Donahoe announced his resignation. As we previously noted about 23andMe, the fact that a big bet doesn't pay off doesn't necessarily mean the bettor was wrong about everything. Donahoe made his decisions in the context of COVID's impact on retail and complicated manufacturing challenges, but the years that followed played out differently than anticipated. That said, even though I initially did not agree with Donahoe's quote about Nike's being of China and for China, because I thought it sounded out of context with the tensions between that country and the United States (and Nike is a quintessentially American company), I came to believe that Donahoe was right to prioritize Nike's strong relationship with China given the revenue and supply-chain dependencies. While I believe he would do several things differently in hindsight, had he known how the world would evolve postpandemic, I can appreciate how he navigated this particular cross-pressure.

Kering: "We Need to Be Relevant in Each Country"

Jeff Immelt has said that there's no such thing as a truly global company; he called GE an American company that did business globally. As GE employees, we could never shed the company's essentially American character or its obligations to the laws and culture of the United States. But if any company provides a counterexample to Jeff's principle, it's Kering.

In chapter 1 we met François-Henri Pinault, chairman and CEO of the Paris-based luxury fashion conglomerate Kering, which owns a lineup of elite global brands including Gucci, Balenciaga, Saint Laurent, Alexander McQueen, and Brioni. All enjoy high consumer awareness, stellar reputations, and premium pricing power—but even those superior qualities don't mean it's easy to lead such a portfolio. Though most of those brands are many decades old, the Kering group itself is fairly young. It evolved from the Pinault family's earlier retail conglomerate, with François-Henri taking over from his father in 2005 and leading a rebranding as Kering in 2013.

Luxury retail is a unique category because a big part of its allure is exclusivity, and by definition you can't (and don't want to) scale exclusivity. Pinault has always resisted the temptation to chase market share growth by reducing production standards or lowering prices. "The thing with luxury brands is that when you reach a high level of visibility and desirability, and you grow fast, you have a risk of overexposure, of banalization of the brand. So the more you are successful, the more you need to elevate the brand to remain very desirable. We need to continue to grow without losing exclusivity."[11]

He noted that each of their luxury brands had a long heritage of quality craftsmanship in their DNA, but that wasn't enough to keep most of them from struggling at some point. "Never forget that Gucci was almost bankrupt in 1993. It began to revive in 1994 and we bought it in 1999. Other brands needed a turnaround as well. Saint Laurent was losing money when we bought it in 2001. Our brands, at least in couture and leather goods, were not clearly positioned in the '80s or '90s in our key markets of America, Western Europe, and Japan."

So how does such a company grow globally and consistently under such constraints and challenges? Pinault described four pillars of Kering's growth strategy since 2013. First is riding the organic growth in demand across the entire luxury sector. Second is creating additional demand for the individual brands by stressing their unique qualities and the creativity of their designers. Third is maximizing the operational value that Kering's central organization brings to supporting each brand, for example via shared logistics and supply chain efficiencies. And fourth is a relentless commitment to talent—to hiring the right creative and business people in the right positions to maximize the potential of each brand. This strategy has worked well so far; since Pinault became CEO in 2005, some of the group's brands have tripled revenues.

The talent pillar is where Pinault personally devotes most of his attention. "It wasn't enough to make beautiful products for everyone—we needed to have a specific creative vision on each brand. This is why between 2012 and 2016, I changed all the creative directors at Saint Laurent, Gucci, Balenciaga, and Bottega Veneta, and more recently at Alexander McQueen. And this is what improved the visibility and desirability of the brands, and will give us the opportunity to continue to scale the entire group. All those brands repositioned on fashion to improve their differentiation and desirability."

It's in this talent area that Kering exemplifies the difficulty of figuring out which decisions are best handled centrally and which are better left to the creatives and business leaders on the ground in the thirty-five countries where the group does business. The group management team is committed to hiring local leaders in every geography, to make it easier to adapt to local cultures. They believe decentralization pays off much better than sending French employees around the world.

As Pinault stressed, "I'm the CEO of the group but not the CEO of any of our brands. I work on the overall strategic vision and priorities for the group. One of the key principles for the group is that we see different market segments that should be covered by different brands. They are not the same and we don't want them to be seen as the same, and not merely by price positioning. We try to avoid any overlap of brands inside the group."

He sees Kering's cross-pressures over geography as inevitable but manageable. "We operate in more than thirty-five countries, all with different cultures. We are dealing with very different customers, so we need to be very global in the way we think. In each market we have local people, but most of our products are uniform around the world. The level of adaptation of most luxury products is very low. It's important to customers that what we sell in New York is the same as what we sell in Shanghai. And most of our brands sell a type of personal luxury that is very much linked to the cultures of France and Italy. In fact, the production is almost entirely done in those two countries."

On the other hand, even truly global products need to be marketed with authentically local messaging. "When it comes to marketing and communication, we adapt the way we tell our brand stories to each local culture. We had to decentralize our communication teams across Europe, Asia, and America, to make our campaigns locally relevant. It's very important to create local attachment in our brand messaging. But it can be very difficult to understand how to reposition a brand to make it relevant in the United States,

South America, China, Korea, and Japan, without losing its consistency. We don't want to be different from one country to another, but we need to be *relevant* in each country. So it's a fine line when we fine-tune our brand stories."

Speaking of China, Pinault considers it one of their biggest challenges and opportunities. The good news is that over the past decade many Chinese consumers have been obsessed with Kering's brands, and an increasing number have the resources to afford their products. On the other hand, fake knockoffs remain a big problem. Meanwhile, Kering has to constantly monitor the evolution of international tensions in the region, against a backdrop of global geopolitical rivalry. The company's executive committee even worked on fictional scenarios of a military conflict in Asia to make sure that contingency plans are reflected and debated in advance, even if they are (hopefully) never needed.

Unlike other issues where headquarters defers to the local management in each market, Kering approaches sustainability from a centralized perspective. It's not just about following the environmental laws of different countries relating to carbon emissions and pollution; it's also about looking beyond legal boundaries to consider the right thing for the planet. "We treat sustainability as a global problem, but it's not the same everywhere. We start from the creative stages of our value chain in every market. When it comes to product development and production, we evaluate every step from raw materials to the supply chain to the customers. For instance, when you look at producing cotton in different parts of the world, we have to consider the cost of water in one region versus another. We need to do our part to make water cleaner."

Kering proves that a global organization can avoid the common tensions between a central headquarters and far-flung outposts. It balances the centralization of operations, product development, and sustainability with the decentralization of sales and marketing to appeal to local tastes. And it prioritizes attracting and retaining talent that can excel in all of those spheres. As a result, a Gucci bag maintains its consistent high quality no matter where you buy one, though the messaging about Gucci's brand promise is idiomatically different from Paris to Athens to Mumbai to Tokyo.

Standard Chartered: "It Doesn't Work Without Financial Intermediaries"

Like Kering, Standard Chartered has deep roots in one country (the United Kingdom) but operations that generate up to 90 percent of its profits in about seventy other countries, especially in Asia, Africa, and the Middle East. In fact, the banking conglomerate has been doing business in some of those areas for nearly 150 years and has deep relationships with many of their local companies. This duality drives a series of geographic cross-pressures for the management team of this financial powerhouse.

Adding to the geographic mix, Standard Chartered's CEO since 2015 has been an American, Bill Winters. He was hired following a distinguished career in banking, including twenty-six years in various leadership roles with J.P. Morgan. Among his connections to the UK, he was the only career banker invited to serve on the Independent Commission on Banking, established by the UK government in 2010 to recommend ways to improve the industry's competition and financial stability. He then served as adviser to the Parliamentary Commission on Banking Standards and led an independent review of the Bank of England's operations. He was even awarded a CBE for his services to the nation's economy in 2013.[12]

Winters arrived during hard times for Standard Chartered. The bank was experiencing unexpectedly large losses "after being pummeled by its exposure to emerging markets and bad loans. . . . The bank posted a pretax loss of $1.52 billion for 2015, compared with a pretax profit of $4.24 billion the year before."[13] As Winters recalls, "I was brought in to lead a turnaround. The bank was broken, and many of my new colleagues didn't even understand how broken it was. I found it hard to trust the insiders who had created the mess."[14] He quickly began replacing key executives with outsiders, starting with a new chief risk officer. Before long, Standard Chartered was making a fresh start with 25 percent new managing directors and 100 percent new members of its C-suite.

His new job forced Winters to become an expert on all aspects of Globalization 2.0. He stressed how valuable it is for companies to hire talent with local expertise when they enter new markets, rather than adopting one-size-fits-all practices. For instance, if Coca-Cola wants to expand into a new country in Africa, it needs a banking partner with a deep understanding of how that country's business community and government work. Standard Chartered markets itself as a mediator between large global companies and unique local markets. And Winters personally views building bridges between individuals, companies, and countries as a vital contribution to the public interest, not merely as a driver of revenue. "While we have a connected world, it doesn't work without financial intermediaries to connect everyone. There's no other way around it, and that's our role."

Financial services are one of the world's most heavily regulated industries, and different countries and regions have broadly conflicting laws, which can create a minefield for a company like Standard Chartered. As Winters observed: "We're the sixth-largest clearer of U.S. dollars, which means that we're a leading policeman for financial crime, money laundering, and sanctions compliance. That's adjudicated by the U.S. Department of Justice, which requires us to have a big U.S. operation. Yet we're still a British bank, fully subject to British laws."

Such potential conflicts are even more complex when they involve the bank's operations in China. "My nightmare is what we call conflicts of law, where one country says you're required to do something, but the other country says you're prohibited from doing the same thing. Take the transmittal of customer data. The U.S. government may say we're required to hand over customer data regarding a Chinese company. But the Chinese government may say it's against the law for us to share that data." Standard Chartered can't afford to alienate either of the world's two biggest economies, so it navigates this minefield with great caution. "We figure out the consequences of violating a law on one side or the other, and if the consequences are minor, we might decide just to suck it up and take it. But we'd first look for reassurance that both sides understand the consequences of the choice we were being asked to make."

Winters says his guiding principle for such cross-pressures is transparency. "Every one of our Chinese customers knows that we will comply with U.S. law as well as Chinese law. And we tell them that if there's a conflict in law, we'll deal with it as transparently as we can. But we'd rather not discuss hypothetical future situations in advance."

One consistent compliance challenge is when major powers impose sanctions on specific countries, companies, or individuals. Winters has found that the U.S. government usually has good reasons to impose sanctions on specific entities within countries such as Iran, Russia, and China. "We're a bank that operates in the U.S. with a U.S. license. It is our job to implement sanctions when imposed, so we do, full stop. But the Chinese also apply sanctions, even on U.S. politicians, and if any of those people or companies are our clients, we also have to recognize those sanctions."

Some issues are more morally nuanced than simply declining to do business with entities under international sanctions. "We see some pretty horrific violations of human rights, but viewed through different lenses, different people get more or less upset about them. When certain people are uniformly bad, we stop doing business with them. But some situations are very tough judgment calls. If I had to rely on my personal views on the human rights of every country and company we deal with, I might end up pulling my hair out."

For instance, Winters feels the cross-pressure between his personal support for LGBTQ people and Standard Chartered's interests in many socially conservative countries. "We're the biggest foreign bank in Uganda, which passed a strict law that made homosexuality a criminal offense—even a capital offense in cases involving minors. The law includes an obligation for witnesses to turn in anyone they suspect of homosexual activity. That couldn't be further away from Standard Chartered's core values or my personal core values." There was some discussion within his management team of pulling out of Uganda to protest that law. But homosexuality was already illegal in nineteen markets where Standard Chartered operated, including Oman, Bahrain, Qatar, Brunei, and Singapore. In some of those countries it was even illegal for Standard Chartered to send employees a message in support of LGBTQ Pride month, or to encourage them to bring their full selves to work.

"We ask the question all the time: Is this bad enough that we need to leave the country? We have left countries like Iran and Afghanistan, but we have not left Uganda or Saudi Arabia. Quite the opposite; we've been investing in Saudi Arabia and we take the view that we can be a force for good there. I'd like to think that our investments and the visibility of our female employees have made a small contribution to the transformation of that society. I hope we can also have some influence on Uganda." Standard Chartered believes that expressing its views privately, with the implication of a potential withdrawal, can be more effective than making grandiose public statements. "We make it clear that the way we allocate capital is influenced by the degree to which we think a country is retrogressive." Winters also devotes a lot of attention to climate change and sustainability, with a focus on encouraging more companies to join carbon markets. "I try to pick my fights. One area I became deeply involved in was a task force for scaling the voluntary carbon markets. Our objective was to grow this currently low-confidence market into something that could channel hundreds of billions of dollars. I really threw myself at that, and it helped establish Standard Chartered as a thought leader in sustainable finance, which I personally believe in deeply."

Navigating through these global issues requires a competency we discussed earlier—leading on nuanced issues in a world that has little appreciation for nuance. Winters is clear on his personal views and values. How he stewards the organization and his employees through these issues is informed by his constant balancing of local and global dynamics.

Axel Springer: How Do You Compete with Free Media?[15]

So far we've focused on Globalization 2.0 cross-pressures within companies that produce physical products (Nike sneakers, Gucci bags) or sell services tied to specific locations (Standard Chartered's expertise and relationships that help companies enter new markets). But such pressures are even greater in industries that have become digital and intangible, such as streaming television and music services, news organizations, movie studios, and video game developers; such companies are far more at risk of being disrupted by new competitors who might be based anywhere in the world.

Mathias Döpfner, CEO of German media conglomerate Axel

Springer, recognized this sobering reality sooner than most of his peers in journalism and entertainment. When he took over the company in 2002, management's strategic goals centered on outperforming their German competitors and selling physical products such as magazines and newspapers. But Döpfner set out to transform this conservative company—launched in 1946, at the dawn of West Germany's postwar rebirth—into a cutting-edge, digital-first leader in global media. He recognized that news, information, and entertainment would surely continue to become increasingly global, which would offer little long-term protection to even the biggest media company in a single market.

Döpfner encouraged his team to stop thinking of their competition as other German media companies; actually, they were competing with any outlet seeking the attention and spending of their many audiences. By the 2010s, it was clear that global tech giants such as Google and Facebook were the biggest threat to content creators like Axel Springer. Search and social platforms tempted media companies with the promise of access to their massive global user bases, from YouTube video watchers to googling news junkies to people sharing article links with their friends. For example, Facebook's news feed drove a significant amount of traffic to Axel Springer's online journalism and entertainment. But Facebook and other tech platforms could use their power as intermediaries to siphon off a lot of the monetization of that traffic. And, with a simple adjustment to their algorithms, the platforms could easily make consumers harder and more expensive to access.

This threat was especially true for Google, which began driving millions of users to Axel Springer content via its Google News aggregator, but delivered far too little revenue to compensate for the cost of generating all those clicks. Many readers were apparently satisfied with free excerpts or summaries of premium content, rather than paying Axel Springer for subscriptions. And increasingly through the 2010s, the company's professional journalists and media creators were competing with amateurs, including pundits with no traditional qualifications on platforms like YouTube and TikTok. Quality alone wasn't enough to compete with free media.

How could Axel Springer remain relevant and strong in this new climate? Following an initial period of strategic repositioning and exploring the media dynamics in several key markets, Döpfner launched an aggressive plan to make the company both more digital and more global. The digital component included challenging Axel Springer's unit leaders to generate half of the company's revenue and profit from digital products within a decade of 2006—at which point less than 1 percent of the company's revenue came from digital products. This required stressing that they shouldn't hold back from digitization by fearing self-cannibalization of existing print products.

Döpfner viewed their globalization strategy as having both a defensive side, to protect their lead in Germany from encroaching competitors, and an offensive side, to monetize Axel Springer's content in more global markets, taking share wherever possible from local incumbents. This component of the strategy required acquiring new media assets in other countries, especially the United States, while expanding existing Axel Springer offerings into new geographies.

The company established a 9 percent stake in the American news site *Business Insider,* then expanded to full control and 97 percent ownership in 2015, for a purchase price of $343 million. Similarly, in 2014 Axel Springer began a joint venture with another popular American news site, *Politico.* This relationship led to a full acquisition in 2021, for more than $1 billion. A third example was the 2016 acquisition of eMarketer; Axel Springer paid $242 million for a 93 percent stake in this provider of high-quality analyses, reports, and digital market data, which would supplement Axel Springer's paid content businesses globally while also providing valuable insights into the American market.

During 2016, the company established a U.S. headquarters in New York to strengthen its collaborations with these and other American media properties. Döpfner also reaffirmed the company's interest in learning from Silicon Valley by continuing various outreach efforts to the tech industry.

In addition to digitizing and globalizing his company, Döpfner sees part of his role as speaking up publicly on controversial issues. For instance, when a German comedian caused an international incident by doing a vulgar sketch making fun of the authoritarian president of Turkey, and even Chancellor Angela Merkel publicly apologized, Döpfner defended the comedian's freedom of speech. He also wrote a 2023 book—*The Trade Trap: How to Stop Doing Business with Dictators*—to wrestle with the conundrum of whether and how to do business ethically in authoritarian countries. His thesis was that Western companies should shun dictators and cut off trade with any country that repeatedly violates Western norms of basic human values.

Döpfner's role as a Systems Leader is captured not only in how he overhauled Axel Springer's product lineup to keep it relevant as a global media company but also in his willingness to stand up for the company's commitments to democracy and freedom. Whereas Bill Winters at Standard Chartered focuses on ensuring that his company can do business globally while obeying local laws, often working behind the scenes on delicate issues, Döpfner manages potential conflicts by being much more public with his points of view. You and your company may find one strategy or the other more effective for your specific international challenges. Whatever approach you choose, the most important thing is thinking through the implications of any strategy for all of your stakeholders, at home and abroad. If you don't proactively wrestle with these issues, the cross-pressures of Globalization 2.0 can leave you at the whim of others—a place no Systems Leader wants to be.

Mubadala: "The DNA of Emiratis Is Trade"

Remember Khaldoon Al Mubarak, managing director of the Mubadala Investment Company, whom we met in chapter 5? He's one of the most globally oriented Systems Leaders I've ever known. During any given week, he might be flying from Abu Dhabi to meetings in London, New York, Silicon Valley, São Paulo, Tokyo, Sydney, Beijing, Delhi, or just about anywhere else on the planet, in pursuit of investment opportunities or to represent his organization or his government responsibilities.

Given the exceptional diversity of his interests and business partners, I was eager to ask Al Mubarak how he balances his global perspective with his local obligations to Abu Dhabi and the UAE, and how he deals with conflicts among his many global allies. When he visited my class in June 2023, his answer was: "The DNA of Emiratis is trade." As a geographically small country, they can only thrive by maintaining productive relationships with just about every other country. This friend-to-all approach has generally paid off. He noted that in the 1970s, Libya and the UAE had very similar GDPs, but now the UAE drives roughly ten times as much economic output as Libya.

A key part of this strategy is not allowing the nation's cordial relations with superpowers to lead to any exclusive alliances, even though both the United States and China would love to forge such arrangements. The United States is the UAE's most important security partner, while China competes with India to be its biggest trading partner. Mubadala can't afford to alienate any of them, or indeed any other significant nation. This is a good example of the difference between the bipolar, us-or-them geopolitics of the Cold War era and the more complex multipolar world of today. Even a relatively small country doesn't have to choose sides permanently. If anyone pressures Mubadala or the UAE to stop doing business with one of their partners, the company and the country will resist that pressure strongly.

However, this doesn't mean that they have to agree with those partners in every situation. Early in the Obama administration, for instance, the UAE's annual trade with Iran was $25 billion. But after the United States applied sanctions against Iran, it dropped to just $4 billion. That was a tough blow for the UAE, but they accepted it as the cost of their relationship with the United States. But then in 2015, after the Iran nuclear deal, the United States canceled most of its Iran sanctions in return for limitations on Iran's nuclear program. Many in the UAE were frustrated by this sudden reversal, which had been made seemingly without any concern for America's allies.

Like other Systems Leaders we've met, Al Mubarak oversees responsible investing policies. He works hard to view challenging situations through other people's lenses as well as his own, believing that most moral conflicts arise from looking through just a single lens. He also distinguishes between *understanding* someone else's perspective and *accepting* that perspective if it conflicts with your own values.

As he put it, "It's normal for me to be pulled right and left. What makes it easier for me to deal with is having a clear set of values that I live by. That set of values usually leads me to an answer, and even if it turns out later to be the wrong answer, I sleep very comfortably with the repercussions. So I try to avoid unnecessary stress by simplifying every issue and pushing it through my values test."[16]

Questions to Ponder

- Much of this chapter is about the dilemma of doing business with and in countries whose behaviors you might find morally offensive. Where do you land on the spectrum between mostly tolerant leaders such as John Donahoe and Khaldoon Al Mubarak, and more critical leaders such as Mathias Döpfner?

- Do you agree with Bill Winters that quiet diplomacy and behind-the-scenes conversations may be more influential in such situations than highly visible public protests or cancellations of deals?

- Do you agree with Jeff Immelt's position that there's really no such thing as a global company? Or does the approach taken by Kering—with its legions of local experts repositioning its brands around the world—prove that it's possible to be a truly global company rather than (in this example) a French company?

- Should Systems Leaders who do business globally treat their home country as just another key stakeholder? Or is that attitude more likely to cause harm than good?

- Have you ever had a situation in which you felt a strong conflict between your obligations to your employees, customers, and investors, versus the best interests of your country? If so, how did you deal with it?

CHAPTER 8

Purpose:
Ambition *and* Statesmanship

The Dearth of Statesmanship[*]

In his 2022 book, *Leadership,* former U.S. secretary of state Henry Kissinger analyzed the traits of six global leaders (Konrad Adenauer, Charles de Gaulle, Richard Nixon, Anwar Sadat, Lee Kuan Yew, and Margaret Thatcher) in the context of their times. Kissinger zeroed in on two attributes in particular, calling them "vital" and "the bridge between the past and the future: courage and character—courage to choose a direction among complex and dif-

---

[*] The words *statesman* and *statesmanship* are intended to describe people of any gender or sex, and are used solely for the purpose of simplicity and to avoid the awkwardness of writing "statesman or stateswoman" over and over.

ficult options, and which requires the willingness to transcend the routine; and strength of character to sustain a course of action whose benefits and whose dangers can be only incompletely glimpsed at the moment of choice. Courage summons virtue in the moment of decision; character reinforces fidelity to values of an extended period."[1]

In its review of the book, *The Wall Street Journal* praised Kissinger for calling out a vacuum in today's leadership—especially that there is a "dearth of statesmen that has left the world misruled by populists and technocrats."[2] It struck me that this same "dearth of statesmanship" applies to today's business leaders as much as it does to political leaders. Both groups require character to figure out the right thing to do in tough times, and courage to act on those values.

After finishing the book, I shared my concern about this leadership void with a colleague. Why did so few of today's business leaders embody the traits captured by Kissinger? We spoke about leaders in the past who modeled these behaviors, and she suggested that business students would benefit from a checklist of the attributes of a statesman or stateswoman. I came up with six:

- Gravitas of personality and purpose

- Intelligence and wisdom about the seriousness of the times

- Dependability in volatile situations

- Moral guidance based on principles and actions, without hectoring or condescension

- Driving change beyond self-interest

- Always showing up when needed—on time and ready to engage

Statesmanship may sound old-fashioned, but it's an essential trait for a Systems Leader to hone. Those of us with a few decades in the business world under our belts have usually encountered at least one senior leader who made everyone sit up straight and speak more eloquently, just by the way they would enter a room. Statesmen and stateswomen still care about their self-interest and ambitions, of course, but never at the expense of their organization's higher purpose. As Stanford professor William Damon put it in chapter 1: "Purpose is an active commitment to accomplish aims that are both meaningful to the self and of consequence to the world beyond the self."

Statesmanship is also a good way to describe the *opposite* of the Musk-Zuckerberg cage match that we discussed in chapter 2. Those two famous and powerful CEOs didn't display any gravitas of personality or purpose, or wisdom about the seriousness of their times. The collision of their ambitions and vulnerabilities caused them to lean into volatile situations rather than counter volatility with dependability. They showed little moral guidance, but plenty of hectoring and condescension. And forget about driving change beyond their self-interest—those taunts and counter-taunts were entirely about their self-interest and ego gratification.

In contrast, Systems Leaders who have mastered the cross-pressure of statesmanship and ambition focus on preserving and improving their organizations for the long run, rather than being overwhelmed by short-term problems. They embrace change and progress while ensuring that the fundamental essence of their culture endures. They don't get thrown off course by chasing the next shiny object that crosses their line of vision.

At the same time, however, Systems Leaders temper their vision for change with wariness about realistic limits—about the ways in which an organization can change without losing its core purpose.

This duality—between aggressiveness and temperance, change and stability, personal ambition and selfless contribution—can make the quality of statesmanship somewhat hard to pin down.

In this chapter we will explore how Systems Leaders handle cross-pressures around their ultimate purpose: Why do they do what they do? How can they rise as far as their talents will take them without stepping on others? Are they dreaming too big, or not big enough? How can they impress people and win respect without coming across as arrogant jerks? And how can they navigate tough times and nuanced, complex problems?

The Systems Leaders we've already met throughout this book give me hope that statesmanship is far from extinct. Those who embody it often keep an intentionally low profile and don't attract much media attention, because they don't drive clicks. But they are out there and well worth emulating.

Solve Problems That Matter

One of my former students, venture capitalist Katherine Boyle, wrote a spectacular 2022 essay, "The Case for American Seriousness," arguing that a general deficit of seriousness was damaging our collective capacity for more effective government policies, international impact, and social programs. While her missive focused on the American experience, I believe her lessons apply globally. "There's a common question in Silicon Valley about what makes an extraordinary entrepreneur.... [To me] the trait that is most meaningful is the hardest to describe. It is the fire in the eyes, the ferocity of speech and action that is the physical manifestation of seriousness.... It is a holy war waged against the laws of physics. It is the burden of having to upend sometimes hundreds of years of entrenched interests to accomplish a noble goal."[3]

She goes on to encourage leaders in both the public and private sectors to ignore mockery in pursuit of big projects that will really make a difference. "Build housing for the middle class. Build schools for the kids who want to learn math. Build next-generation defense capabilities with young people who grew up coding. . . . Cut the red tape that stops us from building infrastructure fast. Build factories in America. Build resiliency in the supply chain. Build work cultures that support mothers and fathers so they can have more children."[4]

Today's Systems Leaders show their seriousness by focusing their time and energy on problems that matter for our species. More than at any time in the past, the leaders of today's companies have the ability to influence industries and spheres of life that touch literally billions of people—from space flight to mobility to health-care to energy. The chance to drive positive change on problems that matter has never been more possible—or more urgent.

Natarajan Chandrasekaran, chairman of India's largest conglomerate, the Tata Group, echoed this idea when he spoke to my class in June 2023: "Society is the purpose of our existence." He argued that it's impossible to do the right thing for your shareholders if you're not equally concerned about your broader community, and relying on that higher purpose to help guide your decisions.

Think back to Naomi Allen at Brightline, who has taken on the huge challenge of reinventing mental health care for children and teenagers. As she told me, "A lot of the people we've hired have a personal mission tied to pediatric mental health, just as I do. That's why they're here."[5] Yet at the same time, as we saw, she is also confronting all the usual challenges faced by any operating executive, including hitting revenue targets, satisfying external partners, and cutting costs when necessary—including via layoffs. She must balance the nobility of her mission with the practical realities of her role.

Leading on Nuanced and Complex Issues

Michael Fullan, former dean of the Ontario Institute for Studies in Education, researched the attributes of leaders who were effective in driving change in struggling K-12 school systems. In his 2019 book, *Nuance: Why Some Leaders Succeed and Others Fail*, he argued that the only way to address challenges as complex as fixing underperforming schools was by appreciating the nuances of many interrelated academic, social, economic, and cultural issues. He described a nuanced leader as one who "learns to grasp how things work, and then helps themselves and others figure out how to make them work better. . . . Any decision that requires judgment, getting people on board, drawing on local knowledge, ingenuity, commitment, etc., requires nuanced leadership that gets beneath the surface to problem solve throughout the process of discernment."[6]

Like educational leaders, business leaders are increasingly confronting delicate social, cultural, economic, and international issues that all require nuance—even as social media and other forces make it increasingly hard to have nuanced discussions. Such issues include race relations, income equality, political polarization, LGBTQ rights, gun violence, climate change, the role of morality in foreign policy, and more. How can any leader provide thoughtful, nuanced insights against the tide of simplistic tweetstorms (Xstorms?) and TikTok rants? And what can leaders do when speaking out on any controversial position could alienate a significant number of employees or customers, but staying silent will also draw criticism?

Given that no individual can possibly navigate all such issues to the satisfaction of all stakeholders, it's essential to clarify and adhere to the purpose of your organization, its core values, and heuristics for thinking through these issues. No heuristic will be perfect in every situation, but at least you'll have a good starting point for applying your purpose and values to extremely tricky situations.

You may recall from chapter 2 the healthcare startup CEO who wrote an article vigorously protesting the overturning of *Roe v. Wade,* only to lose a valued pro-life employee who felt unwelcome and excluded from the company. That CEO's heuristic was to remain silent on most controversial issues, but not on one that would directly affect American healthcare. On the other hand, another of her core values was making all of her people feel valued and included, and she failed in this case to uphold her company's stated value of inclusion. It felt like a no-win situation.

As we'll see in other examples, leading with nuance isn't easy, especially when complex issues create cross-pressures between multiple positive values that, in an ideal situation, wouldn't conflict with each other.

Waste Management: "Whose Brand Is It Anyway?"

Jim Fish is CEO of Houston-based Waste Management, North America's leading provider of trash collection and recycling services, with more than 20 million residential, commercial, industrial, and municipal customers. WM's industry is the opposite of sexy or cool, and it doesn't attract many graduates of leading business schools. But I'm impressed by the way Fish balances WM's business imperatives with its nonfinancial purpose; his empathy for and humility with employees; and his resolve to preserve WM's long-term success and reputation, looking ahead to a future when he will be long retired. He's also exceptional at speaking out on nuanced issues without imposing his views on employees who may disagree. It all adds up to a case study of stewardship and statesmanship.

Since his promotion to the top job in 2016, he has transformed Waste Management by reconciling its financial goals with its mission to serve the public good, in large part via the aggressive adoption of advanced recycling and energy generation methods. Those created a win-win-win: improved profitability; more and higher-skilled jobs for employees; and the satisfaction of fighting climate change by "recovering valuable resources and creating clean, renewable energy."[7] The company now puts sustainability at the core of its public messaging. Its website proudly states: "We're constantly seeking to find the best ways to extract the most value from waste. It's what drives us every day, as individuals and as a company."[8]

As Fish recalled, "Our strategy was to make ourselves synonymous with sustainability. So we bought a couple of smaller companies that could help us. We rebuilt and added artificial intelligence to our recycling plants, which allowed us to increase the volume coming into those plants. Now we're able to process more recyclables at the same number of plants. And on the back end we now produce a better commodity, with less material going to landfill as what we call residual. Advanced optical sorters and AI equipment can do better than humans at maximizing how much gets recycled."[9]

This mission also helps WM improve employee engagement and reduce turnover. "A lot depends on how valued you feel, how appreciated you are, how much of a contribution you can make to the mission, and whether you subscribe to that mission."

Fish's concern for getting employees enthusiastic about the mission dovetails with his empathy. While some leaders may still assume that employees care mostly about money, benefits, and working conditions, he quoted the wisdom of Southwest Airlines founder Herb Kelleher: "Herb said something in his book that stuck with me. If your people feel valued and feel like they're making a difference, because you remind them that they're making a difference, they will be happy in their roles and will want to stay at the company for the long term. And if your employees are happy, your customers are going to feel that happiness. And if your customers are taken care of and feel happy, then your shareholders are also going to be happy."

Fish has used two main tactics to express his empathy and build relationships with more than 42,000 employees. The first is extensive travel to WM's far-flung operational centers. "My father-in-law, who was a pipefitter with a tenth-grade education, told me that great leaders go out to meet their people and really get to know them. That advice strongly influenced how I operate and why I travel to so many locations to meet frontline staff."

His second key tactic is "Fish Food for Thought"—a regular email that he uses to share his views and values with everyone. The topics are often serious, but the language is always simple, straightforward, and modest. He positions himself as a real person who doesn't have all the answers, not an omniscient authority figure. "I want people to understand that my priorities are my Christian faith, my family, and my job, in that order. When I say I'm a Christian, that doesn't mean I'm trying to evangelize at work. But I want my teammates to know exactly who Jim Fish is. I believe everyone needs to set clear priorities for themselves. Yours don't have to be the same as mine, but you need clarity about yours."

Some of his emails are quite emotional, like one announcing the death from cancer of an Ohio route manager. Fish disclosed a special surprise that Waste Management arranged for this Dallas Cowboys fan. "I had never met Tom Miller before June 13, 2018. About two months earlier, Public Sector Rep Vince Crawford reached out to me, telling me about Tom's illness and asking if I could possibly make a trip to Ohio to surprise Tom. . . . To the complete shock of Tom and most everyone else present, I walked into an operations meeting . . . with NFL Hall of Famer and all-time leading rusher Emmitt Smith from the Dallas Cowboys. . . . It was a lot of fun, and it was something that Tom remembered fondly several weeks ago as he was reflecting on his time at WM."[10]

Whenever his emails touch on controversial issues, Fish is careful not to lapse into hectoring or lecturing. For instance, after the Uvalde, Texas, school shooting he wrote: "We all cope with tragedy in our own way. For me personally, it starts with anger as to why we can't seem to stop these types of mass killings. I desperately wish I could stop them. At this time, the only thing I can do is stay firm in my faith. My belief is that we all deserve better, and while God doesn't control all human events, there is a *full* reckoning coming for those evildoers who perpetrate such crimes. I encourage you to leverage our Employee Assistance Program and to support one another in coping with these recent tragedies and finding your own opportunities to influence change in your communities when you feel compelled."[11] Notably, the email doesn't mention his own views on gun regulations.

Fish also threaded a needle in his 2021 email announcing the company's decision not to require WM employees to get the COVID vaccine, at a time when emotions ran high, both pro and con, about vaccine mandates. He wrote in part: "WM will not require our team members to get the COVID-19 vaccine, unless required by a federal, state or provincial government mandate. We'll continue to encourage it and are currently exploring pilot vaccine incentive programs. . . . But at the end of the day, after doing your own research and talking to your own families, I believe that this truly is an individual decision, and you should always do what is best for you and your family. Like me, I'd encourage you to seek your physician's advice."[12]

Fish recalls how he reached that conclusion: "Several people on our board and my senior team put a ton of pressure on me to mandate the vaccine. The way I saw it, if you haven't gotten the shot, you should seriously consider it. But it's still your decision, and your employment will never, as long as I'm here, be dependent on your shot status. You will not lose your job over COVID."

After his "Fish Food" about the vaccine went out, Fish said that it "pissed off some on our board and our senior team. But when I went out in the field and talked to frontline people, so many of them thanked me for letting them make their own decision."

Fish knows that he walks a fine line between living his values and imposing them on the organization. He never wants anyone to think they're being censored or "canceled" for their views. "You and I may have different opinions on something, but if you're at least willing to listen to my opinion, and I'm willing to listen to yours, maybe we'll find some common ground. Or maybe we won't, but we can agree to disagree. But we're in a bad place if the new rule is, 'Here's my view but I don't want to hear yours, and I'm going to prevent your point from coming out.'"

On other issues that don't directly affect WM, Fish resists pressure to speak out. "When I took this position, I fully anticipated competitive pressures and Wall Street analysts being jerks on earnings calls, and hard questions from our board about strategy. What I didn't expect was getting pressured on social issues. I got a call from a big-time CEO I know, asking why I hadn't spoken out on the [antiabortion] Texas Heartbeat Act. He said I should storm into Governor Abbott's office and threaten to move WM out of the state if they didn't repeal it. I replied, first of all, we're not ExxonMobil—if I tried to threaten Governor Abbott, he'd tell me not to let the door hit me on the way out. And second, don't assume you know what I think about that Texas law."

Fish encourages all leaders to show similar restraint on controversial issues, to focus on their responsibility as organizational stewards. He summarizes this principle with a pithy question that I'd recommend as a sign on every leader's desk: "Whose brand is it anyway?" It may feel like your personal brand, but every company is its own distinct entity—even if it's a startup that you founded. And that company may last well beyond one's time as a leader in the organization.

Box: "We're Not Going to Get Drawn into That Debate"

On the surface, it's hard to imagine a leader more different from Jim Fish than Aaron Levie of Box, whom we met a few chapters ago. Their contrasts include Houston versus Silicon Valley; waste collection versus software; a baby boomer upbringing versus a millennial upbringing; and a devout Christian worldview versus a secular worldview. But I was struck by how similar they are in their approach to the purpose and values of their companies. Their similarities help prove that Systems Leadership can span all those differences and more.

Both Fish and Levie consider it essential to protect their employees during tough times, and equally essential *not* to impose their personal views on controversial issues or use their respective brands as a personal soapbox. Both avoid the kind of grandstanding or virtue signaling that we noted in the chapter on unserious behavior. They might have opposite opinions on gun control or *Roe v. Wade*, but they agree that political activism can hurt a company's mission and cohesion.

Sometimes Levie feels pressured to speak out on public issues, just as Fish was pressured about that Texas abortion law. This was never truer than in the first months of the Israel-Hamas war in 2023. "With the Middle East, not saying something was taken as saying something. And saying something to condemn one group but not another did more harm than good. These are very difficult and complicated issues that change constantly. I don't know how anyone can put out a simple statement that seriously addresses those issues and stands the test of time. Whatever you said on October 7 might no longer land on November 14."[13]

Given this complexity, Levie generally avoids making public statements regarding public controversies, except "when we have an intuition that this is so important to our employees, who are really impacted or hurt. I reserve that for only a handful of major topics." One example was personally advocating for gay marriage, an issue that affected many Box employees. But after the Hamas terrorist attacks on Israeli civilians, Levie opted to simply have Box's head of HR send an internal message of empathy and support for Israeli employees affected by the crisis. "We had to make it clear to our employees that we were there for them, but we're not going to get drawn into that geopolitical debate."

If anyone at Box is offended enough to leave because of one of Levie's public statements (or silences), he can live with that. "I don't think I would try hard to convince somebody to stay. I would just tell them it's okay that we have different views, assuming this issue doesn't impact your daily work. We don't need to debate this in the workplace." He believes, for instance, that passionately pro-life people should be able to work comfortably with passionately pro-choice people, and vice versa. And he laments that "society always has to take ideas to their logical extreme, instead of just being reasonable about everything. There are no winners in this current system."

Another striking similarity between Fish and Levie is that both are willing to challenge conventional wisdom on workplace culture. For instance, Levie thinks that accommodations for work-life balance have gone too far in many organizations. At a B2B software provider such as Box, an urgent tech glitch may occasionally require a 10 PM Zoom meeting, or interrupting an expert on the weekend or during their vacation. In such situations, he says, "We have to do everything we can to make sure we deliver for our customers, and I don't really care that you're on vacation." He even advocates for nudging the pendulum back to a somewhat more "Darwinian" workplace. "People who choose to opt in and can work hard and execute without burning out should stay. But if that standard is too hard for you, or this isn't the right place for you, we understand and wish you well. I don't think companies should do too much adaptation for different individuals."

As previously mentioned, I cotaught with Aaron for five years. I always found him to be kind, thoughtful, and welcoming toward students, guests, and staff. He blended youthful enthusiasm and optimism with a realistic, nuanced perspective that rejects any political or business orthodoxy, even when virtually the entire technology industry is in lockstep disagreement.

Graybar: "Leadership Is About Everyone but You"

While interviewing Fish and Levie about these issues of statesmanship, I kept hearing a statement by Graybar's Kathy Mazzarella echoing in my head: "Leadership is about everyone but you." That's often the opposite of how leadership is studied and taught, even at elite business schools, where we tend to encourage students to focus on their own personal development rather than what they can do for others.

As you may recall, Graybar has 9,500 employees in 345 locations, providing equipment to more than 150,000 customers. Because of Graybar's rare structure of employee ownership, its shareholders include many current and retired employees. These shareholders tend to remain exceptionally engaged, often attending retiree reunion events and submitting feedback on what the company is doing or where it could improve. Mazzarella finds it amusing when corporate governance experts debate the tension leaders face between their obligations to shareholders and to stakeholders, because in her case they are mostly the same.

"I get a lot of my energy from knowing I have an obligation to this organization and all the people who work here. It's important that I work as hard as they do. I make mistakes and I don't have all the right answers, but they deserve to have me at my best and giving my best. Otherwise, I'd be failing them. I really don't want to let them down."[14]

This framing of her purpose (and the company's purpose) goes far beyond the importance of hitting Graybar's financial goals. It even goes beyond treating employees well and fostering everyone's personal development. Mazzarella's empathy for her people feeds directly into her concern for the long-term health of the organization, well beyond the forthcoming conclusion of her own tenure. As she observed, "I've been CEO for twelve years and only have a few more years left. So I think a lot about how I want to leave things for the next leadership team, to make sure Graybar is in great shape. We just had a record year and the company is financially strong, but we're facing some headwinds on growth. Although I've been through this before, there are people on my leadership team who haven't experienced tough times. My focus is on educating and preparing them for whatever lies ahead."

Many business leaders love to quote Michael Corleone in *The Godfather*: "It's not personal. It's strictly business." But for a stateswoman like Mazzarella, every official decision and action is extremely personal. "If we underperform, I feel like I'm letting people down. I once asked a good friend, now the CEO of a Fortune 50 company, if he also took things personally at work. He looked at me and said, 'Kathy, if you ever stop feeling, you *are* letting people down, and you should no longer be in your job.' "

Cloudflare: "The World Is Craving Leadership That's Authentic and Principled"

Michelle Zatlyn, cofounder, president, and COO of the internet infrastructure and cybersecurity company Cloudflare, gave my class a different perspective on statesmanship. She and her colleagues use social media and other platforms to promote the company's higher purpose as "cyber stewards," not to promote themselves as individuals. Their communications focus on what Cloudflare stands for, even more than its pitch to B2B customers as a safe and reliable service provider, or its status as a conduit for about 20 percent of global web traffic and a guardian against more than 70 *billion* daily attempted cyberattacks.

Zatlyn has an exceptionally strong commitment to transparency. She told an interviewer that beginning in Cloudflare's early days, circa 2010, "We started to blog about technical problems we were having. People would, in the comments, help us decipher the problem with the code."[15] This started a virtuous cycle that drove customer trust in Cloudflare as a business that actually cared about the public, not just about maximizing profitability. "Bad things would happen; sometimes there would be a security breach. You don't have to talk about these things—in our space, the common approach was not to talk about them. But we felt that to build trust, you need to be transparent. And so we started to be really transparent about why we were building something, or when something went wrong, what happened and what we were doing to fix it."

Cloudflare saw this commitment to transparency sorely tested over an especially complex and nuanced issue: the restriction of highly offensive content. Soon after the Charlottesville white supremacist rally in August 2017, CEO Matthew Prince decided to block access to the neo-Nazi website The Daily Stormer. This was an extremely rare use of what experts call "the death penalty" by an internet infrastructure provider—the first time Cloudflare had taken such an action. Its policy until then, backed up by legal rulings, was that it wasn't responsible for moderating content, just as a telephone company can't be held liable if mobsters plot a murder over the phone. Since Cloudflare had no legal obligation to restrict content, it had always refrained from banning any sites, to avoid opening the door to lobbying and political pressure to keep banning more and more sites.

To address a flood of questions about his decision, Prince turned to the Cloudflare blog: "Our terms of service reserve the right for us to terminate users of our network at our sole discretion. The tipping point for us making this decision was that the team behind Daily Stormer made the claim that we were secretly supporters of their ideology. . . . Like a lot of people, we've felt angry at these hateful people for a long time, but we have followed the law and remained content neutral as a network. We could not remain neutral after these claims of secret support by Cloudflare."[16]

More cautious CEOs might have stopped with that simple explanation. But Prince added that he thought his power to ban an evil site was "dangerous." He feared that concentrating such power at a few big companies, without regulations for deploying it, would encourage vigilante justice. It would turn the internet into a Wild West town where the sheriff might not stop a lynch mob from killing a suspect, depending on the sheriff's whims that day.

He wrote: "You, like me, may believe that the Daily Stormer's site is vile. You may believe it should be restricted. You may think the authors of the site should be prosecuted. Reasonable people can and do believe all those things. But having the mechanism of content control be vigilante hackers launching DDoS [Distributed Denial of Service] attacks subverts any rational concept of justice. . . . At its most basic, Due Process means that you should be able to know the rules a system will follow if you participate in that system. Due Process requires that decisions be public and not arbitrary."[17]

Two years later, Prince again wielded his arbitrary power to stop providing service to 8chan, a racist and anti-immigrant forum that had become an online home for several mass shooters and many of their sympathizers.* Then he again used the company blog to share his reasons for singling out this site from among the 19 million internet properties that Cloudflare protected.

"We do not take this decision lightly. Cloudflare is a network provider. In pursuit of our goal of helping build a better internet, we've considered it important to provide our security services broadly to make sure as many users as possible are secure, and thereby making cyberattacks less attractive—regardless of the content of those websites. . . . We reluctantly tolerate content that we find reprehensible, but we draw the line at platforms that . . . directly inspire tragic events and are lawless by design. 8chan has crossed that line."[18]

I'm not sure I always agree with Prince's views on these questions of free speech versus hate speech and the appropriate role of private companies in making these determinations. But I give him credit for publicly airing his thought processes. In doing so, he was acting thoughtfully and not as an absolute monarch—much as Jim Fish did when wrestling with a potential COVID vaccine mandate.

---

* It has since been renamed "8kun."

Michelle Zatlyn has said that when she cofounded Cloudflare with Prince and Lee Holloway, she didn't really think of herself as a leader. But after a decade of engaging in executive team debates over thorny issues, she came to accept that anyone who starts a company is a leader, whether they embrace that label or not. And any leader's choices "can make an impact on how your business is run and the experience your team has and your customers have, and you should really take that seriously. I think that the world is craving leadership that's authentic and principled."

Can Startups Display Statesmanship, Too?

As we've seen, it's often easier to grasp the advantages of Systems Leadership by looking at counterexamples who behave very differently from Systems Leaders.

In my almost forty years in Silicon Valley, I have never seen any technology explode as quickly as generative artificial intelligence. When ChatGPT launched at the end of 2022, it felt like as big a game changer as the debut of the iPhone in 2007. And since then, generative AI has had an even steeper initial adoption curve than smartphones did, as we saw in chapter 1.

People in countless fields have been scrambling to figure out how they might deploy AI and how it might impact their companies and industries. And media coverage of these innovations has been more polarized than any I've ever seen, ranging from calling AI the greatest technology ever invented[19] to literally the precursor of the end of our species.[20] It's a new Gold Rush, and as we saw during the dotcom frenzy of the 1990s, gold rushes always create temptations to engage in take-the-money-and-run hucksterism rather than statesmanship.

OpenAI, the creator of Chat GPT, has been closely watched by both fans and detractors, who note that its leaders have taken numerous actions that don't appear to be driven by any higher purpose. They often issue statements about public-spirited intentions, but some of their deeds have been too sordid for comfort. I won't give them a free pass on statesmanship just because OpenAI is a startup in the middle of a white-hot field. Even startups have an obligation to take responsibility for any potential negative impact on the world.

Sam Altman, one of OpenAI's original investors, became CEO in 2019. He arrived with what *The Washington Post* called a "polarizing" past: "Before OpenAI, Altman was asked to leave by his mentor at the prominent start-up incubator Y Combinator, part of a pattern of clashes that some attribute to his self-serving approach."[21] In November 2023, he was fired by the board of OpenAI but then quickly returned when the board was disbanded by leading shareholders—a series of moves that drew alarm bells from corporate governance experts. As I write this, the startup's governance structure is still fluid as it explores becoming a for-profit entity, and various machinations have led to turnover among an astounding number of senior leaders, giving Altman even more power.

Meanwhile, *The Wall Street Journal* called Altman out for his massive yet opaque investments in multiple other startups that depended on their relationships with OpenAI. "The 39-year-old oversees an artificial-intelligence startup valued at $86 billion that is spearheading a technological revolution. He owns no stake in the ChatGPT developer, saying he doesn't want the seductions of wealth to corrupt the safe development of artificial intelligence, and makes a yearly salary of just $65,000. Less publicly, Altman is one of Silicon Valley's most prolific and aggressive individual investors, managing a sprawling investment empire that is becoming a direct beneficiary of OpenAI's success. The holdings he controls were worth at least $2.8 billion as of early this year."[22] This web of financial entanglements brings to mind a cynical adage: "No conflict, no interest."

The gold-rush quality of AI has clearly attracted leaders with plenty of ambition but minimal understanding of statesmanship and ethics. As a result, customers of AI services must pay close attention to the incentives and behaviors of their suppliers, as they would with suppliers of any other key resource. Just as you wouldn't trust a partner who sold shoddy products with substantive material defects, or one that you suspected of exploiting your data without your consent, the new AI behemoths should also be subject to caveat emptor.

A Systems Leader running one of these AI companies would focus on the long-term purpose of AI and the moral imperative to provide it responsibly, rather than virtue signaling about the public good while privately focusing on making a quick fortune. The more frenzied everyone around you is acting, the more important it is to take a step back and review the statesmanship checklist.

Questions to Ponder

- Do you agree with Henry Kissinger that statesmanship has fallen out of favor as a benchmark of great leadership? Or is it more likely that most of today's leaders are no better or worse at statesmanship than historic figures like Nixon and Thatcher?

- Would you add any additional attributes to the checklist for aspiring statesmen and stateswomen?

- Do you agree with Katherine Boyle that too many entrepreneurs and politicians are too modest in their ambitions? Should they strive to take on harder challenges that, if solved, could improve the world in more dramatic ways?

- After learning how Jim Fish and Aaron Levie deal with controversial social issues, how do you think you would deploy a platform as visible as theirs? When would you speak out on issues you care about but that don't directly affect your organization? When would you hold your tongue?

- What do you think of Fish's decision to reject the advice of both his board and his senior team to impose a COVID vaccine mandate on Waste Management employees? Was that an appropriate use of a CEO's discretion, guided by his personal commitment to individual liberty? Or an irresponsible decision that hindered important collective action against the spread of a deadly pandemic?

- Do you agree with Levie that it's appropriate to interrupt an employee during his or her weekend or vacation to solve a significant tech glitch, or is that an inappropriate breach of work-life boundaries these days? Put another way, is the purpose of fixing a disruption for your customers more or less important than the purpose of respecting the work-life balance of your team?

- Does Matthew Prince's decision to use his company to ban abhorrent websites, while decrying the fact that he has such power, strike you as statesmanlike or sanctimonious? Or something else?

- Kathy Mazzarella said, "If we underperform, I feel like I'm letting people down." Is that a healthy attitude for a leader, or a recipe for getting too emotional about decisions that ought to be made with stoic logic?

■ Does the cross-pressure between ambition and statesmanship change during a gold rush such as generative AI today, the real estate boom of the 2000s, or the dotcom boom of the 1990s? Is it fair to expect leaders to focus on a long-term purpose when everyone around them is racing to cash in before a bubble pops?

CHAPTER 9

Putting It All Together: Life as a Systems Leader

Now that we've explored the five major cross-pressures one at a time, let's look at how a single Systems Leader in a high-pressure role navigates all five at once, and how these challenges interact with each other. I could have chosen many of my interviewees for this chapter, but I landed on one who taught me, in visceral terms, that Systems Leadership works even during an unprecedented crisis. Michael Dowling is living proof that no matter how tough things get, it's possible to keep your people focused, inspired, and delivering their best possible work—for their own sake, for their organizations, and for the greater good.

Meet Michael Dowling

Dowling has been CEO of Northwell Health, the largest provider of healthcare services in New York State, since 2002. The company was created from the mergers of several hospital systems and adopted its current name in 2015. Organized as a nonprofit integrated healthcare network, Northwell has more than 90,000 employees spread across 21 hospitals, 890 outpatient facilities, the Zucker School of Medicine, and the Feinstein Institutes for Medical Research. It includes 52 urgent care centers, 220 primary care practices, numerous kidney dialysis centers, acute inpatient rehabilitation centers, skilled-nursing facilities, a home care network, a hospice network, and other clinical, academic, and research services. Overall, Northwell cares for more than 2 million patients each year and has a budget of just under $20 billion.

Dowling, who grew up in Limerick, Ireland, still hasn't lost his accent after decades in the United States. He had an academic background in social policy before transitioning to state government and then to healthcare management. Over his two decades as Northwell's President and CEO, he has guided the company through significant growth and expansion, both organic and via acquisitions. He was ranked first on *Modern Healthcare*'s 2022 list of the 100 Most Influential People in Healthcare, which was his sixteenth appearance on that prestigious list.

Dowling excels at seeing all sides of Northwell's highly complex ecosystem, which includes multiple players with competing interests—some profit driven, some nonprofit, some governmental. Providing healthcare can be a low-margin business, especially compared to other ecosystem players such as drug developers and medical device manufacturers. Those companies take much less risk but enjoy much higher profits. Northwell, in contrast, needs to constantly balance value and risk to avoid going into the red, while also avoiding the kinds of risks that might hurt or even kill their patients.

I was aware of Dowling's achievements but didn't fully appreciate his mastery of Systems Leadership until early April 2020, when he spoke to my class during one of the worst weeks of the early COVID crisis. Throughout our class session his cell phone kept ringing because the governor's office kept coordinating with him about the rising death toll in New York. The state faced a dangerous shortage of hospital beds and intensive care equipment, and at that point no one knew just how much worse the crisis would get before it began to improve.

I could only imagine the stress Dowling was under, and I told him we would certainly understand if he had to cancel his Zoom meeting with us. But he kept his commitment to show up for one hundred students on the other side of the country, at 9 PM his time, and did so with full engagement and impressive candor.

In my seventeen years of teaching up to that point, Dowling's session was one of the most powerful moments I had ever witnessed during a class. A leader dealing with suffering and death on a mass scale took the time to explain his business challenges and their greater impact on the world. He helped my students see "leading through uncertainty" not as a theoretical concept but literally as a life-and-death challenge.

American healthcare had already changed tremendously between his hiring as CEO and the onset of COVID, both in technology and in the structural impact of reforms like the Affordable Care Act. Now it was certain to keep changing in many unpredictable ways. So it's ironic that Northwell was depending on the steady hand of a somewhat old-school leader, at least in terms of communications technology.

"People are surprised when I tell them I almost never use a computer. I write notes and memos longhand. If I need to talk to you, I schedule a call or meeting. I don't text. I rarely use email for work; just for mass emails to employees, wishing everyone happy holidays and that sort of thing. If I have a problem with your behavior, I've found that the best way to understand and resolve the issue is face-to-face. I can't do it in an exchange of little paragraphs via email. But that doesn't mean I don't appreciate the benefits of technology. I just want everyone to realize that for every benefit there's a drawback, and leaders need to balance both."[1]

As we take a closer look at Dowling's insights and experiences, I don't want to imply that his approaches to the five cross-pressures are the only valid ways to respond to them. We've met other Systems Leaders who do things quite differently. But Dowling's instinctive strategies have helped Northwell generate consistently strong results for more than two decades, and, to me, he's the epitome of a Systems Leader.

Priorities: Execution *and* Innovation

Dowling intuitively balances Northwell's drive for excellent short-term results and its investments in long-term innovation—even though innovation in a rapidly changing industry can be unclear and full of initiatives that don't work out. For instance, he doesn't pretend to know what American healthcare will look like in ten years. Will the United States begin inching toward a European-style universal insurance system, or will the country repeal the Affordable Care Act and make insurance even more of a free market? Either trend would force Northwell to reinvent itself.

Rather than worry about what might change beyond its walls, Dowling teaches his people to do the best they can with today's environment, while trying to plan ahead for whatever future changes may be required. Even more urgently, they need to anticipate the impact of the rapid expansion of artificial intelligence, telehealth, and other innovations. Dowling foresees both enormous potential and enormous danger as technology reinvents healthcare from the ground up.

"Some people jump at the idea that new technologies will solve the problems of the world. No, they won't. They might be a helping hand in possibly solving some problems. But I think leadership has to determine the right balance between protecting ourselves and taking risks. Our social media has already shown us that we can't simply trust technology all the time."

Facing the cross-pressure to deliver on both execution and innovation, many senior leaders believe the answer is dividing those goals into separate functions staffed by separate teams. But Dowling doesn't organize his people that way, because he believes execution and innovation can't be separated. "A lot of the stuff we do operationally has strategic implications, and how we think about strategy obviously affects our operations. We are all in the business of strategy, because good operational people think about strategy all the time."

On the other hand, Dowling noted that he spends more time today on Northwell's broader mission and strategy and long-term brainstorming, compared to years ago when he spent more time in the operational weeds. He trusts his executives to handle most day-to-day details. "I'm personally thinking about strategy more than about operations, maybe 60/40 at this point. But I'm still very involved in operations because the two are so intertwined."

For instance, one of Northwell's current challenges is applying AI to genomic sequencing and other cutting-edge aspects of medicine. Now that it's increasingly easy to sequence a human genome, there are countless possibilities for improved treatments and diagnostic processes. Scientists around the world are combining genomics with AI to help them develop highly targeted drugs for patients with certain genetic markers. AI is also making huge strides in specialties like radiology, in some cases more accurate in diagnosing early-stage cancers than experienced radiologists.

If Northwell is going to capitalize on such breakthroughs, it will either need to hire many AI engineers or partner with tech companies that can provide the necessary capabilities. This issue goes to the strategic question of which roles are best filled internally (even if it means competing for scarce and expensive talent), and which are best outsourced. At the same time, it's also an issue with serious implications for Northwell's operations. Dowling expects his executives to think about both sides in tandem.

His attitude toward organizational integration flows naturally from Northwell's unique structure. The organization is different from most healthcare systems because its major units are discreet but all interrelated. The biggest is its huge clinical care operation, both inpatient and outpatient, offering every service from birth to end-of-life hospice care. Second is medical education; Northwell is the third-largest medical teaching organization in the United States, with a medical school, a nursing school, and more than two hundred approved training programs. Other key units include medical research, their pharmacy, and a significant community health operation.

Dowling is always looking for new ways to integrate those distinct operations, and his goal is to hire and promote leaders who can innovate on integration. "Our clinical operations are integral to how we teach, and how we teach is integral to how we operate. And what we do in research is integral to the new treatments that we need to deliver operationally."

People: Strength *and* Empathy

Dowling shows deep empathy for all 90,000-plus Northwell employees; to him they are never merely line items on the cost side of a budget. He's equally concerned about the experiences of the patients who depend on them, sometimes literally, for life-or-death treatments and procedures.

During his 2020 presentation to my class, one of his most emphatic messages was that there's no conflict between being a determined, strong, tough-minded leader on the one hand, and acting with empathy and kindness on the other hand. He noted that anyone who equates strong management with coldness is misguided. "The fact that I take a hard line sometimes on people who don't behave properly doesn't mean that I lack emotional intelligence or empathy."

Dowling walks that talk by showing up for his people, even and especially during tough times. Early on in the COVID crisis, he was on the front lines of New York's danger zones with his hospital executives, while also taking frequent calls from the governor's office. Simply showing up is a massive advantage for Systems Leaders, even when they don't have all the answers or have to answer for decisions that have gone wrong. Most employees don't expect perfection from their leaders, but they crave a sense of caring, understanding, and shared sacrifice. They also want to see evidence of resilience—a resolve to do whatever it takes to get the organization through a crisis and into whatever new reality awaits on the other side.

It can take a huge time commitment to build "showing up" into your weekly calendar. Notes Dowling, "I spend an extraordinary amount of time personally with employees. I meet with doctors and nurses and other staff for breakfast every morning at 7:00 AM. Sometimes I'll also meet them for lunch. I'll take twenty-five to thirty frontline employees out to dinner every four weeks." He meets with every new hire—about 250 each week—in small groups. This commitment alone takes two to three hours per week.

In addition to all those group meetings and one-on-ones,

Dowling also does extensive town halls, where he and his top executives encourage honest feedback. "My definition of teamwork doesn't mean that we don't disagree or argue or challenge each other. I like people who offer constructive input. I'm willing to bend and move and change because we work as a collective."

He especially appreciates younger employees, who tend to have different priorities and behaviors and can be surprisingly outspoken about their perspectives, compared to a Baby Boomer like Dowling (or a Gen Xer like me). "I'm receptive to those differences. Being an older person who works with younger people helps keep me young."

He recognizes that the higher you rise in any organization, the less likely people are to tell you the unvarnished truth rather than what they think you want to hear. As mentioned in chapter 3, Carl Ice of BNSF once told my class, "You never lose an argument in your own conference room." This makes it essential to communicate that you really do value honest feedback. Still, Dowling makes a key distinction between constructive and unhelpful criticism. "I enjoy being around people with different opinions, but that's very different from tolerating anyone who is disruptive to the team. I tell our leaders all the time: if you want to have healthy vegetation grow, every so often you've got to weed the garden. And when we weed the garden, we're actually showing empathy to the good plants that we want to grow well. Over time, I have developed less tolerance for people who just complain just for the purpose of complaining, without adding constructive ideas."

Dowling's core beliefs about leadership were shaped by his youthful experiences playing competitive team sports. "Games are won or lost in the locker room. How we talk to each other inside our locker room represents how we perform our jobs." That's why he treats those town hall presentations and Q&A sessions with employees as among his most important activities.

He also noted that while he may modify his language to communicate more effectively with certain audiences, such as frontline employees, senior executives, the board, or the media, he strives to make his fundamental messages and personal style consistent. He believes that projecting empathy must include projecting openness and transparency. Great leaders come across with great consistency—as the same person in good times and bad, and in front of any conceivable audience.

One arena where balancing strength and empathy is especially tricky is when technological or globalization trends make certain employees redundant or too expensive. Leaders who refuse to seriously consider automation or outsourcing will end up wasting money and betraying their obligation to maximize financial results. On the other hand, those who thoughtlessly or even eagerly purge employees when their skills get rusty can destroy workforce morale and engagement. Systems Leaders try to take advantage of cost-saving opportunities without treating their people like replaceable cogs in a machine. Dowling exemplifies this blended path, treating the hiring, training, and career development of Northwell's workforce as a key source of its competitive advantage and one of his highest priorities.

He also spends a lot of time coaching his executives on hiring and other people-related issues. "We are in a relationship-driven business, so if you don't get the relationship piece right, you have a real problem. I teach our managers to hire people with very strong, positive, optimistic attitudes. I'm looking for people who have a high degree of curiosity. I'm looking for people who are people-focused and collaborative in nature. And I'm looking for people who are maximally adaptive and flexible, who can handle discomfort and deal with stress."

Similarly, he puts an unusually strong emphasis on developing and promoting leaders internally. Northwell promotes about

90 percent of its executives from within, in some years as much as
95 percent. It runs comprehensive leadership development programs that stress an entrepreneurial mindset. At any given time,
about 450 Northwell leaders, including physicians, nurses, and administrators, are getting ongoing training, and Dowling tracks
their progress closely.

One goal of this intense leadership development is enabling executive movement throughout different parts of the organization.
A rising star at Northwell might work in the central headquarters
for a year or two, then in ambulatory care, then on the academic
side, then in hospital administration. Dowling believes that such
breadth of experience improves synergy, innovation, and collaboration across business units. It also creates a deep bench of talent
whenever senior positions need to be filled.

I found it enlightening that he sees all the time and effort he
devotes to human resources not merely as an obligation but also as
a joy. "I like being around people. I like walking the floors of a hospital and talking to everyone. That's also why I do an awful lot of
meetings, especially with physicians, over breakfast in local diners.
If I meet you in a diner, I'll get to know you and we can start to
build a relationship. But if you come to my office, that's just a formal meeting. We might solve a specific problem in my office, but I
won't get to know you or lay the groundwork for future conversations. That's a missed opportunity."

However, viewing Dowling as merely a benevolent and extro-
verted boss—one who buys lots of people scrambled eggs and
sponsors their training programs—would be underestimating his
commitment to toughness as well as empathy. His standards are as
high as any other successful CEO's, and he doesn't hesitate to hold
people accountable for violating those standards.

"Twenty years ago, we had to gamble on bringing in executives from the outside, and we made some mistakes because we didn't know them well enough. I had to get rid of some of them, because I won't tolerate people who are not team players. If your behavior shows that you're not a team player, that demonstrates that you don't want to work here. I will gladly oblige you, and you will no longer be working here. If you come into this system and you're a jackass, the system will spit you out."

Ultimately, shaping any workplace culture is a long-term project, a slow aggregation of many small but consistent actions that build trust and collaboration. "You can't change the mindset of a large group right away. You have to prepare to keep at it for a long time. I've found that transforming a hospital to have a culture of teamwork and success can take as long as seven to ten years. Some leaders take over an organization and think they can transform the culture in a year. That's almost always impossible. You have to commit to a long-term plan. You can't get fed up with having to say the right things over and over for years."

Sphere of Influence: Internal *and* External

Even the biggest, most vertically integrated company depends heavily on outside partners. The higher you go in any organization, the more attention you will need to focus externally on the challenges and opportunities posed by suppliers, distribution partners, customers, and regulators. Dowling blocks plenty of time on his schedule to deal with external issues and constituencies. "I have experience in government, in insurance, and in academia, so I can speak their language. A leader's job has to be both inside and outside. What you do outside helps inside, and what you do inside helps outside."

He told my class that Northwell's workforce includes three

thousand people whose primary job is working with insurance companies to make sure the company gets paid for services rendered to patients. Amazingly, about 25 percent of all insurance claims are initially denied. Talk about a "frenemy" relationship with key partners!

Many of Northwell's employees are unionized, so good relations with national union representatives are essential, as are relations with state and federal officials who regulate unions. Likewise, any hospital system has to deal with the intractable challenge of providing emergency care for the indigent, who often show up at emergency rooms without health insurance. If the government requires hospitals to provide emergency care to everyone, dealing with the cost implications also requires good relationships with government regulators and policymakers.

The intersection of politics and public policy affects the leaders of many kinds of businesses and nonprofits, not merely those in healthcare. Not long ago, business leaders were rarely expected to speak out on controversial issues such as abortion, gun control, LGBTQ rights, or wars. But, as we've seen, many employees now want to know exactly where their leaders and companies stand on such issues, with the implied corollary that they don't want to work in a place that offends their personal values.

Dowling strives to balance the expectation that he'll speak out on controversies with the risk of offending some of his stakeholders. "I believe very strongly that leaders should not be afraid to take positions on complex social issues. For instance, I am very active on the gun violence issue and was one of the first CEOs to go public on it years ago. I'm also very involved in sustainability and climate change, immigration issues, veterans' issues, and education."

He recognizes that all these controversies affect his people, whether directly or indirectly, and therefore it's understandable for them to want Northwell to take public positions on them. "For instance, the way I see it, all 90,000-plus of our employees are immigrants—the only difference is whether they're first-generation immigrants, like me, or more removed from that experience. They're all affected by sustainability and climate change. They all have an interest in reducing gun violence. So my external work on these issues helps boost employee engagement."

At the same time, like a good statesman (see the "Purpose" section on page 205), he's mindful that not everyone at Northwell agrees with his positions, and some might be sufficiently offended that they'll want to leave. "The key to avoiding trouble is that I stay at a high level. On immigration, for example, I talk about how we need intelligent talent from every conceivable group of people, if we're going to be as good as we can be. We all benefit from immigration, and we can all learn from each other. But I don't talk about which specific policies we should put in place at the border. On gun violence, I talk about awareness and education and promoting safety, which almost everyone supports. I do not talk about the Second Amendment, which would cause deeper divisions."

Dowling added that in his private discussions with politicians he gets into the details on such issues, but not in his public comments. As a result, he has generated minimal negative feedback within Northwell and very little from outsiders, even though Northwell's operations are in areas that vary widely from liberal to conservative. "Most employees want to be part of an organization that promotes the good of the community, not just the success of the business. When you talk about external issues that connect with people, they feel that sense of belonging."

Geography: Local *and* Global

You might assume that any healthcare system is a strictly local business, because you can't outsource the work of New York doctors and nurses to Asia. But Northwell actually faces many decisions about which functions and supply chains they choose to keep local and which they choose to globalize. For instance, think about how many products those 21 hospitals and 890 outpatient facilities require during their normal course of operations. A difference of a few pennies per unit on bandages or rubber gloves can add up very quickly.

Dowling tries to balance the bottom line with his loyalty to New York and the United States. Unlike most health systems, Northwell has only a single group purchasing organization (GPO) to handle the supply chains for all of its divisions. In addition to generating economies of scale, the GPO also saves money by purchasing all of Northwell's goods directly from manufacturers, rather than depending on distributors. The company also operates two large warehouses to minimize shortages—a key advantage that was a literal lifesaver during the shortages of many medical products during COVID.

Northwell's sophisticated team of supply chain experts must balance multiple mandates:

- To get the best possible value on goods purchased

- To diversify sourcing so there's not too much reliance on any single country. (They overindexed on Chinese imports before COVID, much less so now.)

- To maintain acceptable quality, rather than defaulting to cheap but shoddy products

- To work with companies that can deliver efficiently and meet deadlines

- To purchase locally as much as possible, to promote American companies, especially those based in New York State and/or minority-owned

Dowling believes there's no inherent conflict between taking advantage of global supply chains, supporting local producers, and finding the sweet spot between high quality and low costs. Furthermore, he treats globalization as including far more than the nuts and bolts of supply chains. He sees Northwell's overall mission and community as global, since global events and health trends affect everyone. One of their units is a center that promotes global health, and another does charitable work in local communities. "It's not an either/or situation. It may not be very obvious to people on a day-to-day basis, but our company is part of a global family. If we were discussing this thirty years ago, it would be very different. But today I can pick up the phone and call friends in Singapore, and it's no different than talking to someone in the same building. So it's hard to be disconnected in an interconnected world, and it makes no sense to think of a local community as totally differentiated from the global community."

Globalization is not going away, no matter how much certain isolationists and "antiglobalists" might wish otherwise. The continued advancement of communication and collaboration tools enables and encourages global interconnectivity. All business leaders need a sophisticated strategy for balancing their local and global interests.

Purpose: Ambition *and* Statesmanship

Dowling's approach to public policy advocacy dovetails with his desire to lead Northwell with gravitas and seriousness of purpose, but without hectoring or lecturing. He is hugely ambitious about the company's growth and results, and his own personal success, but never at the expense of his values. That's one definition of statesmanship.

The most powerful part of Dowling's discussion with my class came in response to my assertion that Northwell is not collecting sufficient profits in return for the risks they take, because people die when they get things wrong. When he took over the discussion, Dowling asserted that Northwell could be substantially more profitable if it served only wealthy patients. But what kind of society would that choice create, he asked rhetorically. Profit is only one way to define value, and arguably *not* the most important way.

"Because Northwell is a not-for-profit, my shareholders include my physicians, my patients, and my employees. So my obligation is to all of them. I enhance their shareholder value by promoting health overall. Obviously, I still have a financial responsibility as CEO. We raise money in the bond market, and I meet with the bond rating agencies all the time. We need to maintain our good credit. But even the folks at the bond rating agencies care about an issue like gun violence. They actually compliment me for speaking publicly about it."

Dowling knows that the backlash against corporate activism can equal social media poison, as we saw during the Bud Light controversy of 2023.[2] He also knows it's easier for a business leader to talk about gun violence in New York than about illegal immigration in Texas or transgender rights in Florida. But statesmanship sometimes requires taking controversial stands for the greater good.

"Many leaders at the moment, especially our political leaders, are toxic. The signals they send to our kids are undeniably damaging. Many are basically saying that it's okay to have grievances about everything, to play the victim about everything, and anyone who disagrees must be evil. I'm disgusted with that whole mindset. We need to model civility and decency. Just because you disagree with somebody doesn't mean you can't like the person."

Whether he's negotiating one-on-one in his office or speaking on a public stage, Dowling tries to deal with everyone with that kind of decency and respect. "I love an old Irish saying: The definition of diplomacy is the ability to tell a person to go to hell in such a way that they look forward to the trip."

He added that we need more leaders to model and encourage a sense of civil community, and if politicians can't rise to that challenge, business leaders have to fill the vacuum. "I think too many of them are afraid to speak out or get involved in broader societal issues. They stick to the view that a business leader's sole mission is to grow shareholder value. I disagree completely with that. We all live in a community, and we all benefit from how healthy that community is, both at the organization level and as a society. If we lose a sense of community and mutual interdependence, we're only as strong as our weakest link."

I asked Dowling who he admires these days as a leadership role model who embodies statesmanship. His immediate response was not a healthcare leader or any other business leader, but President Volodymyr Zelensky of Ukraine.

"I got to spend time with him because Northwell is treating a lot of Ukrainian soldiers, especially amputees. When he was in New York to address the United Nations, Zelensky came to one of our hospitals and spent a long time with his wounded soldiers. He drove an hour in the rain from Kennedy Airport because thanking those soldiers, and our hospital staff, was so important to him. To me, that's the essence of great leadership. He understands what's truly important to building morale. Leaving aside whether he's a good military leader or not, his behavior proves that he's 100 percent with his people, and they all know it. It's even more impressive when you consider that he's a former comedian who suddenly became a president, and then a wartime president. And he rose to that huge challenge."

Going further back into history, Dowling also spoke of his

admiration for statesmen like Martin Luther King Jr., Nelson Mandela, and Mahatma Gandhi. Like Zelensky, those icons also rose from humble origins on the strength of their personal integrity and moral authority—not via impressive job titles or wealth. "We don't have many leaders like that anymore. Or if we do, they're not as visible as they need to be."

"Everybody's Watching You Set Those Priorities"

When I asked Dowling if he had any final thoughts about the cross-pressures that sometimes pull him in different directions, his response was a pretty good mission statement for Systems Leadership:

"I think good leadership is about balancing everything we've been talking about. Internal versus external, strategy versus execution, local versus global, short-term versus long-term, and more. It's also about risk versus safety. It's about control versus influence. In each case it's not about going one way or the other, but about how do you straddle both? It's often easier to be just one way. But the trick of leadership is being able to straddle both ways."

As an example of managing internal conflicts, he talked about the debates that arise during Northwell's annual budgeting process. Every business unit and department has their preferred projects that they want funding for. The C-suite's challenge is usually *not* about choosing good projects over bad projects but about prioritizing multiple opportunities that might all be worthwhile—and having no way to be certain how any of them will turn out. Inevitably, even the best leaders will sometimes make the wrong call. When that happens, all you can do is correct it as soon as possible and move forward, and try not to let it shake your confidence.

He also noted that many leaders have a detailed process for budgeting money but not for budgeting their time. "The way you allocate your time sends a huge signal about what you think is important. So you've got to be thinking: Am I spending most of my time on stuff that *used to* matter, or on stuff that *will* matter in the future? Because as you get more senior, everybody's watching you set those priorities."

Finally, he observed that leaders shouldn't expect or pine for some hypothetical future when the pressures of leadership will subside—when their work will become a series of tranquil, sunny days. "I tell my executives all the time that we should never say we're 'successful.' We have had many successes, and we'll have many more. But once you call yourself successful, you're encouraging complacency. You're implying that you don't need to keep growing and learning and developing. We'll never be permanently successful. I worry about getting too comfortable."

Some Takeaways from Dowling's Case Study

As I said earlier, I'm not claiming that Michael Dowling is the ultimate role model for navigating all the cross-pressures we've explored in this book. We've met other Systems Leaders who deploy very different strategies and tactics. For instance, some use texting as a powerful tool for nurturing relationships, as an alternative to Dowling's diner breakfasts, hospital walk-arounds, and small group chat sessions.

With that caveat in mind, Dowling remains a powerful example for how all these issues can interact and overlap during the day-to-day life of a Systems Leader. His efforts to balance Northwell's priorities of innovation and execution inform the way he mandates hiring and training, how he deals with both internal and

external stakeholders, how he addresses globalization and its consequences, and how he juggles his personal ambitions, his goals for
the company, and his wider responsibilities for public health and
the public good. Everything affects everything else.

A crisis such as COVID separates truly great leaders from those
who may buckle under extreme pressure. But it's also in such crises
that the steady accumulation of thousands of small actions and
years of consistent messaging can really pay off. By 2020, Dowling
had built up eighteen years of goodwill by consistently showing up
for his people and having their backs. They trusted his decisions in
unprecedented situations and put in exceptional effort and overtime, even amid frightening uncertainty about how bad the crisis
would get.

I assume that no one reading this will ever end up leading a
huge healthcare network during the onset of a deadly global pandemic. But, if anything, that's all the more reason to study and
(where possible) emulate Dowling's strength, empathy, and clarity
of purpose. If he could develop those attributes and hold on to
them during a time like the spring of 2020, so can the rest of us in
the face of less dramatic challenges.

Questions to Ponder

- How do you split your time between strategy and
  execution? Should you consider making any adjustments?

- When interacting with others, do you tend to show more
  strength or empathy? Why?

- What gets more of your attention—items external or
  internal to your company? How are these two spheres
  connected to each other?

- What is the relationship between the location in which you work and other parts of your country or world? Do you understand and actively manage these interrelationships?

- What pressures do you feel to balance being ambitious and leading as a statesman or stateswoman? In which area do you feel more comfortable? Why?

You Can Do This

The Parable of the Crab

Crabs, like all crustaceans, periodically need to shed their shells in order to grow. When that time comes, they develop new, bigger shells via a process called molting. In fact, crabs *need* to molt their shells because their hard outer barriers get chips and parasites—they actually function less well over time.

After a fracture opens in its old shell and a crab literally backs out of it, something astounding happens: "During this time, the crab is extremely vulnerable . . . and will bury itself in the sand to avoid detection. Once the [new] shell starts to harden (which can take several days) . . . the crab will consume enough food to restore its fat reserves and replace the excess water in its shell with muscle. Then the cycle starts all over again."[1]

When I first encountered an article about this process, I was especially struck by this sentence: "During this transition the crab temporarily transforms from a hard, vicious predator into a soft, paranoid coward that's extremely vulnerable to other predators."[2] It hit me that this is a perfect parable for humans. Repeatedly throughout our lifetimes, we all have to let go of roles and habits that once protected us and made us successful. If we don't shed them, we won't be able to grow and evolve further. But if we do shed our old shells, we have to make ourselves terrifyingly vulnerable during a period of transition. Neither option is ideal, but we all have to pick one or the other.

The older we get, the harder it becomes to shed our old shells. It's only human to want to keep using the skills that made us good at what we do—skills that previously earned us recognition, raises, and promotions—even if they aren't useful anymore. So we stay too long at jobs where we've stopped learning. We remain in dysfunctional workplaces. We stick to careers and industries in decline, rather than pivoting to potentially brighter opportunities. We ignore or mock new technologies rather than embracing or at least accepting the future.

Such resistance is common even among extremely smart and accomplished leaders. Consider Microsoft CEO Steve Ballmer, who said in 2007, "There's no chance that the iPhone is going to get any significant market share."[3] Or IBM president Thomas J. Watson, who said in 1943, "I think there is a world market for maybe five computers."[4] It's easy to laugh in hindsight at such extreme misjudgments, but at the time those were beliefs shared by people with high levels of accomplishment and authority.

As we wrap up our exploration of Systems Leadership, I want to acknowledge that many of the mindsets and practices we've been discussing can be daunting, even a little scary. Many will leave you vulnerable to criticism, especially if you work in a field where the default approach to leadership is the exact opposite. Whether you lead five direct reports, a business unit of fifty, or a corporation of fifty thousand, you may be hesitant to break the mold of "how we do things around here" or your own tried-and-true way of doing things. Such fears are common and understandable. But if you want to rise to your full potential as a leader, you have no choice but to molt your shell from time to time and take your chances during a risky transition.

"You Have to Be Able to Rise Above It"

One of my mentors, Julie Wainwright, taught me a lesson early in my career: "When times get tough, people get real real" (she even named one of her companies The RealReal). In moments of extreme stress and pressure, people show you who they really are and what really matters to them. It's one thing to be visionary, optimistic, generous, and benevolent when everything is going well, and everyone loves you. But the true test for any Systems Leader is what happens when things go off the rails. Can you stay calm and focused? Can you maintain your priorities and clarity of purpose?

I was at Intel in 1994 when a math professor discovered a modest bug in the "floating-point unit" of our flagship product, the Pentium processor chip. When performing certain advanced numeric calculations, the Pentium would return slightly incorrect results several places after the decimal point. The vast majority of PC users would never experience an error, even if they were scientists doing high-level work. In fact, *Byte* magazine estimated that only one in 9 *billion* calculations done with those chips would produce inaccurate results.[5]

But if the technical problem was modest, the PR problem was the opposite. The tech media pounced on the Pentium bug, and before long many mainstream media outlets were challenging Intel's reputation for building high-quality products. Some even compared the situation to the Tylenol poisoning crisis of 1982, in which seven people died—an absurd comparison for a glitch that most users would never even notice. I remember going home for Thanksgiving in 1994 when my grandfather said, "Robert, I saw your company in the news. I'm sorry things are so messed up there." This was from a man who didn't follow tech news (he ran an egg factory for most of his working life), but even he knew that Intel was being raked over the coals.

I watched our famously tough and brilliant CEO, Andy Grove, shift his position from dismissing this minor glitch as no big deal to taking full public responsibility for it. A few weeks after the furor began, we offered to replace every defective Pentium chip for every customer who wanted a new one—an offer that forced Intel to take a $475 million hit to our earnings that year (equivalent to over $1 billion in 2025). Andy faced a lot of heat from the entire tech industry for needing to do the first-ever recall of a computer chip. I watched him process his anger at the unfairness of the situation, including many ignorant attacks on both his own leadership and the integrity of his beloved company.

But Andy didn't let his anger throw him off course. He knew he had to swallow his pride and accept a big loss to save the company, so he did. He led the entire staff through the crisis by keeping our spirits up. He told us that we would get through this adversity and move forward to better days. And we believed him—in part because we all knew his background as a Hungarian refugee who had twice escaped death, from the Nazis during the Holocaust and from the Soviets during the Hungarian Revolution. Those early traumas gave Andy an unshakable sense of perspective, courage, and determination that helped make him an exceptionally effective leader.

The Pentium catastrophe led Andy to write one of the most admired business books of all time, *Only the Paranoid Survive,* so he could share his lessons (and mistakes) with other leaders. I was lucky enough to be tapped by Andy to conduct research for that book, and so I had a front-row seat to watch him as he turned a profound business problem into an opportunity to teach others how to be resilient in tough times.

About two decades later, I had another ringside seat as another tough and brilliant CEO, Jeff Immelt, also saw his stellar reputation take a beating. After decades of steady growth, GE's financial performance and stock price stagnated during his tenure due to a wide range of economic pressures, historical structural decisions at GE, operating missteps, and broader trends in a variety of GE's markets. The same pundits who had previously hailed Jeff as one of the world's greatest executives now trashed him for alleged incompetence and a couple of badly timed acquisitions. He was pressured into retirement in 2017.

When Jeff started coteaching with me at Stanford the following year, he was still getting vilified in the press in very personal terms. I once asked how his skin was thick enough that he didn't get rattled by an attack on the cover of *The Wall Street Journal* or *Fortune*. He replied, "I don't have thick skin. It hurts. But one of my mentors taught me that you have to be able to rise above it."

I share these stories not to solicit sympathy for two extremely successful leaders, neither of whom would ever ask for sympathy themselves. My point is that Jeff, like Andy, accepted the lows as well as the highs of his exalted position. Jeff never vented or whined publicly about the unfairness of those articles. On the contrary, he repeatedly offered to resign from Stanford if we thought he had become too toxic to teach at the university. He never wanted his troubles to reflect badly on the institution. But I was certain that our students benefited tremendously from Jeff's experiences, including the bad ones. He hadn't done anything illegal or immoral; he'd just faced an extremely public reckoning during one of the hardest eras for one of the world's largest companies.

The guest speakers who came to our class—senior leaders who knew how hard it is to make huge decisions with limited information—still universally respected Jeff. Many of them privately voiced concerns to me about how he was holding up and publicly praised him to our students with sincere enthusiasm. In his memoir, *Hot Seat,* Jeff observes that "It's your peers who promote you."[6] It's also your peers who will determine your reputation in the long run, after today's problems fade into history.

I believe Jeff was even more impactful as a teacher because he had gone through hard times; he was well qualified to help new leaders prepare for their own inevitable crises and failures. He was also living proof that any of us can do so many things right yet still have moments of failure. Any of us can be derailed by bad timing or forces beyond our control, as well as by our own mistakes. The big questions in those scenarios: How can you keep going and continue to lead effectively? Can you put the good of your organization ahead of your own ego or wounded pride? Can you accept that your people are not expecting perfection from you, only honesty and positive, forward progress?

A Systems Leader's Checklist

As you set out to apply Systems Leadership, here are a few essential principles to keep handy, based on themes that have emerged throughout this book.

Leader, know thyself. As far back as the ancient Greek philosophers, wise people have known how important it is to understand and work within their own strengths and weaknesses. This capacity separates Systems Leaders from others who react to challenges and provocations impulsively. An aphorism taught at GE's Crotonville Center has stuck with me for many years: "Leadership is the ability to constrain a response to a given stimulus." You may recall that my greatest strength (my passion) is also my biggest weakness, and it took me years to stop sending counterproductive "flame emails" to colleagues who provoked my wrath. My struggle to constrain that response was difficult but essential. I'm not as good as I need to be, but I am better than I used to be.

Do the hard jobs yourself. You are never too senior or too important to get your hands dirty and model hard work for your team. This might include physically hard work, such as at a startup when everyone needs to load boxes onto a truck to make an urgent deadline for a customer. More likely, it will include emotionally hard work, such as deciding who will be laid off as part of an urgent cost reduction, and then telling the affected people directly. Don't delegate such tasks to HR; even if a major layoff requires an experienced HR team to execute, you can volunteer to lead that team and communicate to everyone personally.

Be brave enough to say, "I don't know." Many leaders find it painful to feel ignorant, underprepared, or vulnerable. Yet, especially during a crisis, it's important to remember that no one has all the answers. It is okay to admit (both to yourself and your people) that you are not in control of what's happening, and you need the team to work together to determine the best path forward. You want people to see you as a truth seeker, not a savant with all of the answers. Great leaders (especially startup founders) have a fierce desire to *get it right* but not necessarily to *be right.*

Listen to internal teammates you can trust. Leaders are often bombarded by suggestions and opinions, especially when serious trouble is brewing. It can be extremely tough to know which internal people you should trust. In my experience, while many mistakes stem from failing to listen to internal experts, others stem from listening to colleagues who are dead certain yet utterly wrong.

Your mission is to surround yourself with a diverse team whose credibility is well established and who aren't afraid to disagree with you—respectfully but, when necessary, firmly.

Find trusted partners outside the company. This is a corollary of acknowledging what you don't know and being cautious about who you trust internally. Your peers, direct reports, and even your bosses will often be inclined to tell you what you want to hear rather than share uncomfortable truths you *need* to hear. This problem only gets worse as you become more senior in an organization. That's why trustworthy outside voices who understand your challenges are invaluable. Consider reaching out to former mentors, teachers, members of your board, or friends at other companies (as long as you're not sharing material nonpublic information, of course).

Hold two truths at once. Jeff often refers to the two essential truths that leaders must hold at the same time: Things can always get worse, yet there are always huge opportunities. Be wary if you find yourself believing only one of the two. Relentless pessimism will bring everyone around you down, but relentless optimism will make people question your grasp of reality. As Ecclesiastes, "the preacher," wrote (and Ernest Hemingway titled one of his books), "The sun also rises." No matter how good things are now, prepare for a challenging future. And no matter how bad things are now, take heart that bad times don't last forever.

Watch where you spend your time, because the people who report to you are watching. There's no clearer way to signal to everyone what you consider important than how you spend your days. No matter what adversity you're facing at any moment, you still control your own calendar. Others will try to seize chunks of it against your will, perhaps literally, by sending unsolicited calendar invitations. Find the courage to push back and block time for whatever activities will create the most impact. For instance, if your best leverage comes from talking with your people, make it a priority to protect time on your calendar for critical interactions. (You probably don't have to be as extreme as Michael Dowling, who blocks out a ton of time for small group breakfasts and dinners, one-on-ones, and town halls to solicit feedback, but you do need to make time to listen.)

Be mindful of the difference between skill and luck. As I said early in the book, I'll bet there have been times in your career when you succeeded because you were highly qualified, with the skills to make a valuable contribution to an organization. And there have probably been other times when you were simply lucky to be in the right place at the right time. The first thirty or so people hired at Google became wealthier than they could possibly imagine simply by holding on tight during that rocket launch. But their inordinate wealth had little connection to their contributions, no matter how valuable they were. I like to say that it's better to be lucky than good, and it's even better to be both. It will greatly help your perspective if you can acknowledge times when your luck mattered more than your skills. If nothing else, it will bring an awareness that the things you did during your lucky moments are not necessarily the playbook you should copy in the future. You actually have no idea if those previous actions were the ideal things to do in those situations.

Ask yourself if you'd rehire yourself today for your current job. I learned this concept from Stitch Fix founder Katrina Lake. She told my class that every year or two she asked herself and her leadership team: "If you were hiring for your job today, would you hire yourself? Are you the best person for the role now, rather than when you first got the job? If you're no longer the best person, what are you going to do about it?" Such conversations are a powerful way to drive personal and professional development. But beware that they can be quite uncomfortable, especially if someone was outstanding when they reached their current position but now needs new skills for changing times.

Remember: You Have Free Will

Stanford neurobiologist Robert Sapolsky stirred up a flurry of conversations with his 2023 book *Determined: A Science of Life Without Free Will*. His thesis is that we humans don't really understand the "why" of most of our actions and decisions. What we consider free will is, he argues, some combination of instincts driven by evolution and chemical triggers. For instance, he reduces falling in love not to a magical spark of connection with someone else's personality, intelligence, or even physical attractiveness, but to how much we might simply enjoy another person's smell. (For the record, I really like how my wife smells. But the coefficient of that variable is quite small compared to the many other attributes that have drawn me to her for three decades.)

Even if Sapolsky is right that we underestimate the impact of evolutionary biology—the extent to which we're guided by subconscious imperatives to do whatever will help us survive and reproduce—I remain a stubborn believer in free will. My main counterargument: If there's no free will, why would anyone choose to be a teacher? If everyone's outcomes and decisions were predetermined, teachers would have very little impact on students, which I *know* isn't true.

Most of us who stick with this profession see it as a higher calling—a deeply satisfying opportunity to give students the tools they need to be successful and to make a difference to their families, communities, companies, and countries. This sense of a higher calling also applies to sports coaches. Consider basketball icon Doc Rivers, whom the NBA named one of the fifteen greatest coaches in the league's history.[7] Interviewed for a documentary, Rivers said, "Some of the advice when I first got started was wrong. I was told, 'Don't get too close to [players] because some of them will let you down.' Get close to them! Some do let you down, but so what? Your job is to coach them and make them better players, better people, and better teammates. How to be tough, how to be compassionate, how to be a good winner, and how to be a good loser. . . . I always tell them, 'I am not going to coach you to who you are. I am going to coach you to who you should be someday.'"[8]

Like Rivers, I embrace the joy of helping people become the best possible versions of themselves. And I believe my students have the free will to become whatever sorts of leaders they choose to be. Kind or bombastic? Empathetic or hard-assed? Ambitious or lazy? Working humbly to improve the world, or trying loudly and selfishly to grab the spotlight? The type who arranges for an NFL Hall of Famer to visit a sick employee, or the type who challenges a rival to fight in a cage match? All of those options and many more are open to them after learning about Systems Leadership—and to you, too, dear reader.

At least for now, science can't conclusively resolve my debate with Sapolsky one way or the other. Nevertheless, I urge you to join me in believing in free will, now that you've encountered Systems Leaders who have intentionally chosen how to steward their organizations. I hope you will remind yourself that how you act and react at any given moment is your choice. Your leadership style is not preordained, no matter what your mentors once taught you or what your bosses modeled early in your career.

Acting like a Systems Leader will feel hard sometimes, perhaps even impossible. But if you've gotten this far in this book, I have faith that you can incorporate these principles and strategies into your daily life. Just remember that you are not alone in accepting the higher calling of leading with gravitas, empathy, nuance, resilience, honesty, statesmanship, ambition, and all the rest.

You can do this.

ACKNOWLEDGMENTS

In the summer of 2017, I was in New York meeting with Beth Comstock, then one of GE's Vice Chairs. Beth had been a guest several times in one of my courses and was among the most insightful leaders I'd ever hosted. As we wrapped up an interview for a case study I was writing, Beth said, "As you know, Jeff is leaving GE. He's thinking about what to do next. Would you be willing to chat with him for an hour?"

"Um, sure, Beth. I think I can find an hour on my calendar for Jeff Immelt." Her simple question ultimately led to this book, for which I'm grateful.

A month later, Jeff and I met for coffee at the Coupa Café at the Stanford GSB. He greeted me with a big smile, as if I were a long-lost friend. Truth be told, I had met him only three times before, when I was a junior executive at GE. He had spoken at a couple of training courses I attended at Crotonville, and he once visited one of our work sites when I was present. There's no way he remembered me from those times—I wasn't that important. Nonetheless, Jeff could not have been warmer when we met at Stanford. He explained that he was interested in teaching as part of his next professional chapter, then casually handed me two detailed documents with potential ideas for courses. One was about his learnings at GE, which became the foundation for his book, *Hot Seat*. The other was about systems thinking in the context of leadership.

"That's it," I immediately thought.

At the time I was already teaching four courses, including "The Industrialist's Dilemma," which explored how organizations need to evolve in a world where every product and service was connected, digital and physical markets were merging, and change was happening faster than ever. Jeff's idea of exploring leadership in the context of these same trends fit my interests perfectly. Over the next two years of coteaching, we jointly developed the principles of Systems Leadership.

Then COVID hit. We quickly evolved our (now virtual) course to focus on crisis leadership, since there's nothing like a global pandemic to challenge one's approach to people, priorities, ecosystems, geography, and statesmanship. As the pandemic abated, we further expanded the curriculum to address the latest challenges leaders faced, including geopolitical instability and even more rapid technological change.

All of which is a long way of thanking Jeff for our eight years of close collaboration. I will be eternally grateful to my colleague, friend, and mentor for all of his support. This book simply would not exist without him.

As he did for my previous book, Will Weisser helped me find a way to write the way I speak so I could capture my voice and passion in print. I cannot think of a more valuable thought partner and collaborator. He has become a trusted confidant and teammate.

I am very thankful to David Drake, Paul Whitlatch, Katie Berry, and the entire team at the Crown Currency imprint of Penguin Random House. Their input and support through the writing and editing process have been incredible. I especially appreciate their embrace of the ideas of Systems Leadership and their willingness to discuss these challenges in the context of their own industry.

My literary agent, Eric Lupfer, constantly pushed me on the ideas behind the book, and I benefited from the way he forced me to think more deeply and clarify my messages.

The Systems Leaders who sat with me for interviews were also invaluable in shaping this book. I can't thank them enough for their time, their unique stories, and their thought-provoking insights.

To the many guest speakers and students who have participated in Systems Leadership classes since their first iteration: thank you for your honesty, your willingness to debate hard and controversial topics, and your tolerance for my provocations in the classroom. Just as it's a false choice to believe that leaders can be ambitious or kind but not both, I believe that a challenging, effective course can also be fun. My greatest professional joy is learning together with talented students from every continent and the global leaders who graciously share their time with us.

Finally, the foundation of my existence is my family. My profound thanks to my grandparents, my parents, my sister, my aunts and uncles and cousins, and above all to my wife, Debbie, and our children, Kelly, Evan, and Samantha.

I know exactly from where I come.

NOTES

Chapter 1: The Perfect Storm of Chaotic Forces

1. Christopher Zara, "Gen Xers and Older Millennials Really Just Want to Go Back in Time to before the Internet Existed," *Fast Company*, June 14, 2023, https://www.fastcompany.com/90909279/gen-xers-and-older-millennials-really-just-want-to-go-back-in-time-to-before-the-internet-existed.
2. Zia Muhammad, "Generative AI Is Growing Faster than the Smartphone," *Digital Information World*, August 19, 2023, https://www.digitalinformation world.com/2023/08/generative-ai-is-growing-faster-than.html.
3. Andy Beckett, "The Age of Perpetual Crisis: How the 2010s Disrupted Everything but Resolved Nothing," *The Guardian*, December 17, 2019, https://www.theguardian.com/society/2019/dec/17/decade-of-perpetual-crisis-2010s-disrupted-everything-but-resolved-nothing.
4. Nassim Nicholas Taleb, *The Black Swan: The Impact of the Highly Improbable* (New York: Random House, 2007).
5. *Financial Times* Editorial Board, "Who Wants to Be a Modern CEO?," *Financial Times*, December 26, 2023, https://www.ft.com/content/1a63c186-5f46-4dac-b273-c9e41de6b002.
6. Ibid.
7. Quotes from Anne Wojcicki are from my interview with her in November 2023, edited for length and clarity.

8. Jason Fried and David Heinemeier Hansson, *Rework* (New York: Crown Currency, 2010).

9. Steven Tweedie, "Wayfair CEO Tells Employees the Company Is Profitable Once Again—but to Expect Long Hours and 'Blending Work and Life,' " *Business Insider,* December 13, 2023, https://www.businessinsider.com/wayfair -profitable-again-ceo-email-frugal-work-long-hours-2023-12.

10. Noam Scheiber and Julie Creswell, "Why Is Howard Schultz Taking a Starbucks Union So Personally?," *The New York Times,* December 11, 2022, https://www.nytimes.com/2022/12/11/business/howard-schultz-starbucks -union.html.

11. Howard Shultz, *Pour Your Heart Into It: How Starbucks Built a Company One Cup at a Time* (New York: Hyperion, 1997).

12. From my interview with Revathi Advaithi in August 2023, edited for length and clarity.

13. Quotes from Charlie Scharf are from my interview with him in October 2023, edited for length and clarity.

14. From my interview with François-Henri Pinault in October 2023, edited for length and clarity.

15. Milton Friedman, "A Friedman Doctrine—The Social Responsibility of Business Is to Increase Its Profits," *The New York Times,* September 13, 1970, https://www.nytimes.com/1970/09/13/archives/a-friedman-doctrine-the -social-responsibility-of-business-is-to.html.

16. William Damon and Anne Colby, "Education for a Purposeful Life," in *Education: A Global Compact in a Time of Crisis,* ed. Marcelo Suárez-Orozco and Carola Suárez-Orozco (New York: Columbia University Press, 2022), 181–92.

Chapter 2: Unserious Behaviors in a Serious World

1. Daniel Henninger, "The Musk vs. Zuckerberg Cage Fight," *The Wall Street Journal,* August 9, 2023, https://www.wsj.com/articles/the-musk-vs-zuck -cage-fight-tech-business-media-ceo-fight-ufc-meta-facebook-twitter-x -11853966.

2. Jo Constantz, "From Topless Massages to Private Flights: CEO Mishaps of 2023," *Bloomberg News,* December 28, 2023, https://www.bloomberg.com /news/articles/2023-12-28/elon-musk-mark-zuckerberg-sam-altman-top -wildest-ceo-moments-of-2023.

3. Alexandria Ocasio-Cortez (@AOC): "If Republicans are mad they can't date me they can just say that instead of projecting their sexual frustrations onto my boyfriend's feet. Ya creepy weirdos," X, December 31, 2021, 2:35 p.m., https://x.com/AOC/status/1477000469318885385.

4. Lauren Goode, "Elon Musk Just Told Advertisers, 'Go Fuck Yourself,' " *Wired,*

November 29, 2023, https://www.wired.com/story/elon-musk-x-advertisers
-interview.

5. "Old Man Yells at Cloud," Know Your Meme, Literally Media Ltd., updated
    August 2024, https://knowyourmeme.com/memes/old-man-yells-at-cloud.

6. Laura Curtis, "Remote Work Doesn't Seem to Affect Productivity, Fed Study
    Finds," *Bloomberg,* January 16, 2024, archived January 16, 2024, at
    Archive.today, https://archive.ph/1waXO#selection-4905.0-4905.16.

7. Krysten Crawford, "Study Finds Hybrid Work Benefits Companies and Em-
    ployees," *Stanford Report,* June 12, 2024, https://news.stanford.edu/stories
    /2024/06/hybrid-work-is-a-win-win-win-for-companies-workers.

8. Brian X. Chen, "Apple Is Doing Its Part to End Green Bubble Shaming. It's
    Our Turn," *The New York Times,* November 29, 2023, https://www.nytimes
    .com/2023/11/29/technology/personaltech/apple-iphone-android-bubbles
    .html.

9. CRV, "F*CK TRUMP," Team CRV, *Medium,* August 24, 2016, https://medium
    .com/crv-insights/f-ck-trump-691946de213.

10. Ibid.

11. Ibid.

12. Marcel Schwantes, "Warren Buffett Says You Can Ruin Your Life in 5 Minutes
    by Making 1 Critical Mistake," Inc. (website), November 6, 2021, https://www
    .inc.com/marcel-schwantes/warren-buffett-says-you-can-ruin-your-life-in-5
    -minutes-by-making-1-critical-mistake.html.

Chapter 3: A Better Alternative: Systems Leadership

1. Robert Siegel, "Optimizing Market Structure—Carl Ice, CEO BNSF Railway,"
    Systems Leadership, *Medium,* May 31, 2018—https://systemsleadership.io
    /optimizing-market-structure-carl-ice-ceo-bnsf-railway-924142008521.

2. "Context," Dictionary.com, accessed September 14, 2024, https://www
    .dictionary.com/browse/context.

3. Tom Fairless, "China, Once Germany's Partner in Growth, Turns Into a Rival,"
    The Wall Street Journal, updated September 17, 2020, https://www.wsj.com
    /articles/china-once-germanys-partner-in-growth-turns-into-a-rival-116003
    38663.

4. Zach Barnett, "Nick Saban Explains Why He's Developed a Softer Touch with
    Players in Recent Years," Footballscoop, July 19, 2022, https://footballscoop
    .com/news/nick-saban-explains-why-hes-developed-a-softer-touch-with
    -players-in-recent-years.

5. Amir Goldberg et al., "Fitting In or Standing Out? The Tradeoffs of Structural
    and Cultural Embeddedness," *American Sociological Review* 81, no. 6 (2016):
    1190–1222, https://doi.org/10.1177/0003122416671873.

6. "AI and analytics," Nokia (website), accessed September 14, 2024, https://www.nokia.com/networks/ai-and-analytics.

7. Sameer B. Srivastava et al., "Enculturation Trajectories: Language, Cultural Adaptation, and Individual Outcomes in Organizations," *Management Science* 64, no. 3 (2017): 1348–64, https://pubsonline.informs.org/doi/10.1287/mnsc.2016.2671.

8. Andy Grove, *Only the Paranoid Survive* (New York: Currency/Doubleday, 1996), 126.

Chapter 4: Priorities: Execution *and* Innovation

1. Mark Walker and James Glanz, "Alaska Airlines Flight Was Scheduled for Safety Check on Day Panel Blew Off," *The New York Times,* March 12, 2024, https://www.nytimes.com/2024/03/12/us/politics/alaska-airlines-flight-door.html.

2. Taylor Romine, Sara Smart, and Gregory Wallace, "Tire Falls Off United Airlines Flight Immediately after Takeoff in San Francisco, Damaging Several Cars," CNN, updated March 8, 2024, https://www.cnn.com/2024/03/08/us/united-airlines-plane-loses-tire/index.html.

3. David Gelles, " 'I Honestly Don't Trust Many People at Boeing': A Broken Culture Exposed," *The New York Times*, January 10, 2024, https://www.nytimes.com/2020/01/10/business/boeing-737-employees-messages.html.

4. James Surowiecki, "What's Gone Wrong at Boeing," *The Atlantic,* January 1, 2020, https://www.theatlantic.com/ideas/archive/2024/01/boeing-737-max-corporate-culture/677120.

5. Charles A. O'Reilly III and Michael L. Tushman, "The Ambidextrous Organization," *Harvard Business Review,* April 2004, https://hbr.org/2004/04/the-ambidextrous-organization.

6. Robert A. Burgelman, "A Model of the Interaction of Strategic Behavior, Corporate Context, and the Concept of Strategy," *The Academy of Management Review* 8, no. 1 (1983): 61–70, https://doi.org/10.2307/257168.

7. Mark Gardiner, "The Pan America Marks a New Era for Harley Davidson," *The New York Times,* May 31, 2021, https://www.nytimes.com/2021/05/31/business/harley-davidson-pan-america.html.

8. Susan Carpenter, "An Electric Harley Loses the Growl but Still Aims to Turn Heads," *The New York Times,* August 8, 2019, https://www.nytimes.com/2019/08/08/business/harley-davidson-livewire.html.

9. All quotes from Jochen Zeitz are from my interview with him in September 2023, edited for length and clarity.

10. Harley-Davidson, Inc., "Harley-Davidson Unveils the Hardwire Five-Year Strategic Plan; Targets Profitable Growth and Brand Desirability," *PR Newswire,* February 2, 2021, https://www.prnewswire.com/news-releases/harley

-davidson-unveils-the-hardwire-five-year-strategic-plan-targets-profitable
-growth-and-brand-desirability-301219919.html.

11. Carpenter, "An Electric Harley Loses the Growl."

12. "Timeline," Accenture (website), accessed September 15, 2024, https://www
.accenture.com/us-en/accenture-timeline.

13. "About Our Company," Accenture (website), accessed September 15, 2024,
https://www.accenture.com/us-en/about/company-index.

14. Fortune Media (USA) Corporation, "Fortune Reveals the 100 Most Powerful
Women in Business," *PR Newswire,* October 5, 2023, https://www.prnewswire
.com/news-releases/fortune-reveals-the-100-most-powerful-women-in
-business-301947947.html.

15. *The Industrialist's Dilemma: Julie Sweet, CEO of Accenture North America,*
Stanford Graduate School of Business, February 28, 2019, YouTube video,
4:28, https://www.youtube.com/watch?v=BxYdT84S3pw.

16. Stephen Wilmot, "Tech Consultants Are the New Mad Men," *The Wall Street
Journal,* November 9, 2018, https://www.wsj.com/articles/tech-consultants
-are-the-new-mad-men-1541765256.

17. Interview with Julie Sweet, February 2024, edited for length and clarity.

18. Some background on Boubyan Bank is adapted from Laila AlJasem, William
Barnett, and Robert Siegel, "Boubyan Bank: Driving Digital Banking in the
Middle East," Stanford Graduate School of Business, 2020, https://www.gsb
.stanford.edu/faculty-research/case-studies/boubyan-bank-driving-digital
-banking-middle-east.

19. Ibid.

20. Ibid.

21. Ibid.

22. Rolfe Winkler, "23andMe's Fall from $6 Billion to Nearly $0," *The Wall Street
Journal,* January 31, 2024, https://www.wsj.com/health/healthcare/23andme
-anne-wojcicki-healthcare-stock-913468f4.

23. Robert E. Siegel, *The Brains and Brawn Company* (New York: McGraw Hill,
2021), 23.

24. Siegel, *The Brains and Brawn Company,* 26.

25. Winkler, "23andMe's Fall from $6 Billion to Nearly $0."

26. Ibid.

27. Siegel, *The Brains and Brawn Company,* 29.

Chapter 5: People: Strength *and* Empathy

1. Jane Nicholls, "Inside Crotonville: GE's Corporate Vault Unlocked," *GE News,*
October 29, 2017, https://www.ge.com/news/reports/inside-crotonville-ges
-corporate-vault-unlocked.

2. Joseph A. Schumpeter, *Capitalism, Socialism and Democracy* (New York: Harper and Brothers, 1942).
3. "Essential Elements of Employee Retention," Lynchburg Regional SHRM (blog), October 29, 2017, https://lrshrm.shrm.org/blog/2017/10/essential -elements-employee-retention.
4. Heather E. McGowan, "Learning Is the New Pension," *Forbes,* October 29, 2019, https://www.forbes.com/sites/heathermcgowan/2019/10/29/learning-is -the-new-pension.
5. Ibid.
6. Lindsay Ellis and Ray A. Smith, "Your Co-Workers Are Less Ambitious; Bosses Adjust to the New Order," *The Wall Street Journal,* December 31, 2022, https://www.wsj.com/articles/your-coworkers-are-less-ambitious-bosses -adjust-to-the-new-order-11672441067.
7. Interview with Julie Sweet, February 2024.
8. Sarah Perez, "Amazon Invests $700 Million to Retrain a Third of Its US Work-force by 2025," *TechCrunch,* July 11, 2019, https://techcrunch.com/2019/07/11 /amazon-invests-700-million-to-retrain-a-third-of-its-u-s-workforce-by-2025.
9. Ibid.
10. Amazon Staff, "9 Free Skills Training Programs That Help Amazon Employees Land Higher-Paying Roles," About Amazon (website), Amazon.com, Inc., updated August 15, 2024, https://www.aboutamazon.com/news/workplace/our -upskilling-2025-programs.
11. "€82 Million Injected into UM6P Endowment (formerly OCP Foundation)," *Africa Business+,* updated January 1, 2023, https://www.africabusinessplus .com/en/814501/ocp-e82-million-injected-into-um6p-endowment.
12. All quotes from Revathi Advaithi are from her interview with me in August 2023, edited for length and clarity.
13. Details provided by Flex, May 2024.
14. "About Graybar," Graybar (website), revised June 2024, https://graybar.widen .net/s/pkjrpv2k6f/graybar_factsheet.
15. All quotes from Kathy Mazzarella are from my interview with her in September 2023, edited for length and clarity.
16. All quotes from Khaldoon Al Mubarak are from my interview with him in August 2023, edited for length and clarity.
17. Chip Cutter, "GE Sells Crotonville, a Training Ground for Generations of Managers," *The Wall Street Journal,* April 14, 2024, https://www.wsj.com/real -estate/commercial/ge-sells-crotonville-campus-13fd35a0.
18. Suzy Welch, "Crotonville and the Death of Fun at Work," *The Wall Street Journal,* April 16, 2024, https://www.wsj.com/articles/crotonville-and-the-death-of-fun-at-work-ge-young-employees-office-culture-5ae016ab.

Chapter 6: Sphere of Influence: Internal *and* External

1. Lynda Bourne and Derek H. T. Walker, "Visualising and Mapping Stakeholder Influence," *Management Decision* 43, no. 5 (2005): 649–60, https://doi.org /10.1108/00251740510597680.
2. Robert A. Burgelman, *Strategy Is Destiny: How Strategy-Making Shapes a Company's Future* (New York: Free Press, 2002).
3. Calvin Wankhede, "How Does Google Make Money from Android?," *Android Authority,* February 12, 2023, https://www.androidauthority.com/how-does -google-make-money-from-android-669008.
4. Robert E. Siegel, "Hand-Eye Coordination: Organizing Ecosystems," in *The Brains and Brawn Company* (New York: McGraw Hill, 2021).
5. Ibid.
6. Ibid.
7. David Pierce, "Google Is Combining Its Android and Hardware Teams—and It's All about AI," *The Verge,* Vox Media, April 18, 2024, https://www.the verge.com/2024/4/18/24133881/google-android-pixel-teams-reorg-rick -osterloh.
8. Siegel, "Hand-Eye Coordination."
9. Ibid.
10. All quotes from Charlie Scharf are from my interview with him in October 2023, edited for length and clarity.
11. "The Last Thing We Need Right Now Is a Vision Statement," FS (website), accessed September 15, 2024, https://fs.blog/vision-statement.
12. "About the President," University of Montana, accessed September 15, 2024, https://www.umt.edu/president/about.
13. Quotes from Seth Bodnar are from his guest appearance with my class in April 2020.
14. "Brightline," Brightline (website), accessed September 15, 2024, https://www .hellobrightline.com.
15. All quotes from Naomi Allen are from my interview with her in September 2023, edited for length and clarity.
16. Wesley M. Cohen and Daniel A. Levinthal, "Absorptive Capacity: A New Perspective on Learning and Innovation," *Administrative Science Quarterly* 35, no. 1 (March 1990): 128–52, https://www.jstor.org/stable/2393553.
17. Ron Miller, "Aaron Levie Leads Box into Its Third Era Focused on Workflow Automation and AI," *TechCrunch,* March 16, 2024, https://techcrunch.com /2024/03/16/aaron-levie-box-workflow-automation-ai.
18. All quotes from Aaron Levie are from my interview with him in November 2023, edited for length and clarity.

Chapter 7: Geography: Local *and* Global

1. Stephen Hiltner, "Saudi Arabia Tourism: Surprising, Unsettling, Surreal," *The New York Times*, June 5, 2024, https://www.nytimes.com/2024/06/05/travel/saudi-arabia-tourism.html.

2. "Total Stimulus for the COVID-19 Crisis Already Triple That for the Entire 2008–09 Recession," McKinsey & Company (website), June 11, 2020, https://www.mckinsey.com/featured-insights/sustainable-inclusive-growth/chart-of-the-day/total-stimulus-for-the-covid-19-crisis-already-triple-that-for-the-entire-2008-09-recession.

3. Robert Siegel and Lucy Montgomery, "CrowdStrike: On a Mission to Protect," Stanford Graduate School of Business, 2021, https://www.gsb.stanford.edu/faculty-research/case-studies/crowdstrike-mission-protect.

4. C. Todd Lopez, "In Cyber, Differentiating between State Actors and Criminals Is a Blur," U.S. Department of Defense, *News*, May 14, 2021, https://www.defense.gov/News/News-Stories/Article/Article/2618386.

5. "John Donahoe, President & CEO," Nike, Inc. (website), accessed September 15, 2024, https://about.nike.com/en/company/people/john-donahoe.

6. Sara Germano, "Nike Races to Keep from Losing Ground to More Nimble Rivals," *Financial Times*, January 13, 2024, https://www.ft.com/content/e83d7cf5-5752-469e-bdf2-659bc5c92c1c.

7. Shoshy Ciment, "Nike's New Silicon Valley CEO Has Big Plans. Can Nike Follow Through?," *Business Insider*, March 29, 2021, https://www.businessinsider.com/inside-nike-restructure-layoffs-dtc-resale-digitalization-2021-3.

8. Germano, "Nike Races to Keep from Losing Ground."

9. Sara Germano, "Nike Chief Executive Says Brand Is 'of China and for China,'" *Financial Times,* June 24, 2021, https://www.ft.com/content/704a065d-f07d-4577-8133-7db3eb529299.

10. Gabrielle Fonrouge, "Nike CEO John Donahoe Says Breaking Up with China Would Be 'Disastrous' amid Rising Geopolitical Tensions," CNBC, updated May 23, 2023, https://www.cnbc.com/2023/05/23/nike-ceo-john-donahoe-says-decoupling-from-china-would-be-disastrous.html.

11. All quotes from François-Henri Pinault are from my interview with him in October 2023, edited for length and clarity.

12. "Bill Winters, CBE," Standard Chartered (website), accessed September 15, 2024, https://www.sc.com/en/people/bill-winters.

13. Amie Tsang, "Standard Chartered Posts a $2.36 Billion Loss for 2015," *The New York Times*, February 23, 2016, https://www.nytimes.com/2016/02/24/business/dealbook/standard-chartered-results.html.

14. All quotes from Bill Winters are from my interview with him in September 2023, edited for length and clarity.

15. This section is informed by Stanford GSB's Case Study no. 610: Robert A. Burgelman, Robert Siegel, and Ryan Kissick, "Axel Springer in 2016: From Transformation to Acceleration?," Stanford Graduate School of Business, 2016, https://www.gsb.stanford.edu/faculty-research/case-studies/axel-springer-2016-transformation-acceleration.
16. From my interview with Khaldoon Al Mubarak, August 2023, edited for length and clarity.

Chapter 8: Purpose: Ambition *and* Statesmanship

1. Henry Kissinger, *Leadership: Six Studies in World Strategy* (New York: Penguin Press, 2022), xv.
2. Walter Russell Mead, "Kissinger Sees a Global Leadership Vacuum," *The Wall Street Journal*, December 26, 2022, https://www.wsj.com/articles/kisssinger-sees-a-global-leadership-vacuum-world-order-peace-power-civilization-universities-depth-11671990402.
3. Katherine Boyle, "The Case for American Seriousness," The Free Press (website), April 18, 2022, https://www.thefp.com/p/the-case-for-american-seriousness.
4. Ibid.
5. From my interview with Naomi Allen, September 2023.
6. Michael Fullan, *Nuance: Why Some Leaders Succeed and Others Fail* (Thousand Oaks, CA: Corwin, 2018), ix–x.
7. "WM 101," WM (website), accessed September 15, 2024, https://investors.wm.com/why-invest/wm-101.
8. "BUILDING TODAY, FOR TOMORROW® | WM 2024 Sustainability Report," WM (website), accessed September 15, 2024, https://sustainability.wm.com.
9. Unless otherwise noted, quotes from Jim Fish are from my interview with him in October 2023, edited for length and clarity.
10. Jim Fish, "Fish Food for Thought," Substack, January 9, 2020.
11. Jim Fish, "Fish Food for Thought," Substack, May 25, 2022.
12. Jim Fish, "Fish Food for Thought," Substack, August 30, 2021.
13. Quotes from Aaron Levie are from my interview with him in November 2023, edited for length and clarity.
14. Quotes from Kathy Mazzarella are from my interview with her in September 2023, edited for length and clarity.
15. Quotes from Michelle Zatlyn are excerpted from Michelle Zatlyn, "Cyber Stewards," interview by Holly Rose Faith, *Greymatter by Greylock*, April 19, 2022, https://greylock.com/greymatter/cyber-stewards, and edited for length and clarity.
16. Matthew Prince, "Why We Terminated Daily Stormer," The Cloudflare Blog,

Cloudflare, Inc., August 8, 2017, https://blog.cloudflare.com/why-we
-terminated-daily-stormer.

17. Ibid.

18. Matthew Prince, "Terminating Service for 8Chan," The Cloudflare Blog,
Cloudflare, Inc., August 5, 2019, https://blog.cloudflare.com/why-we
-terminated-daily-stormer.

19. Tom Gerken, "Bill Gates: AI Is Most Important Tech Advance in Decades,"
BBC, March 21, 2023, https://www.bbc.com/news/technology-65032848.

20. Matt Egan, "AI Could Pose 'Extinction-level' Threat to Humans and the US
Must Intervene, State Dept.-Commissioned Report Warns," CNN, updated
March 12, 2024, https://www.cnn.com/2024/03/12/business/artificial
-intelligence-ai-report-extinction/index.html.

21. Elizabeth Dwoskin and Nitasha Tiku, "Altman's Polarizing Past Hints at
OpenAI Board's Reason for Firing Him," The Washington Post, updated November 22, 2023, https://www.washingtonpost.com/technology/2023/11/22
/sam-altman-fired-y-combinator-paul-graham.

22. Berber Jin, Tom Dotan, and Keach Hagey, "The Opaque Investment Empire
Making OpenAI's Sam Altman Rich," The Wall Street Journal, June 3, 2024,
https://www.wsj.com/tech/ai/openai-sam-altman-investments-004fc785.

Chapter 9: Putting It All Together: Life as a Systems Leader

1. All quotes from Michael Dowling are from my interview with him in October
2023, edited for length and clarity.

2. Amanda Holpuch, "Behind the Backlash against Bud Light," The New York
Times, November 21, 2023, https://www.nytimes.com/article/bud-light
-boycott.html.

Conclusion: You Can Do This

1. "Molting Crabs, Explained," Seaside Signal, August 23, 2019, https://www.sea
sidesignal.com/news/molting-crabs-explained/article_159d821a-c5d7-11e9
-b0af-77c7de66eb5f.html.

2. Ucluelet Aquarium, "The Crabs Aren't Dead," Ucluelet Aquarium (website),
August 22, 2019, https://uclueletaquarium.org/the-crabs-arent-dead.

3. Luke Dormehl, "Today in Apple History: Steve Ballmer Freaks Out and
Stomps an iPhone," Cult of Mac, September 11, 2024, https://www.cultofmac
.com/apple-history/apple-history-steve-ballmer-iphone-freakout.

4. Jadek & Pensa, "'I Think There Is a World Market for Maybe Five Computers,'" Lexology, September 20, 2017, https://www.lexology.com/library/detail
.aspx?g=164a442a-1b90-49e3-895d-4c54bb49ecce.

5. Tom R. Halfhill, "The Truth behind the Pentium Bug," BYTE, March 1995, ar-

chived February 8, 2006, at the Wayback Machine, https://web.archive.org /web/20060209005434/http:/www.byte.com/art/9503/sec13/art1.htm.

6. Jeff Immelt, *Hot Seat: What I Learned Leading a Great American Company* (New York: Avid Reader Press, 2022), 54.

7. "NBA 75: Top 15 Coaches in League History Revealed," NBA.com, February 8, 2022, https://www.nba.com/news/nba-75-top-15-coaches-league-history.

8. Doc Rivers, *The Playbook,* season 1, episode 1, "Doc Rivers: A Coach's Rules for Life," directed by Josh Greenbaum, aired September 22, 2020, on Netflix, https://www.netflix.com/title/81025735.

INDEX

Note: Page references in *italics* indicate photographs.